The Jewish Sabbath

The Jewish Sabbath

A Renewed Encounter

(*Formerly titled* Shabbat Shalom)

by

Pinchas H. Peli

Schocken Books New York

 Published in the United States by Schocken Books Inc., New York, and simultaneously in Canada by Random House of Canada Limited, Toronto. Distributed by Pantheon Books, a division of Random House, Inc., New York. Originally published as *Shabbat Shalom: A Renewed Encounter with the Sabbath* by B'nai B'rith Books, Washington, D.C., in 1988.

Grateful acknowledgment is made to the following for permission to reprint previously published material:
"The Sabbath in the Bible" from *Sabbath—The Day of Delight* by Abraham E. Millgram, Jewish Publication Society, 1944.
"Shabbat—A Key to Spiritual Renewal in Israel" from *Judaism, A Quarterly Journal of Jewish Life and Thought,* Vol. 31, No. 1, Winter 1982.
"Sabbath: A Hassidic Dimension" from *Perspectives on Jews and Judaism, Essays in Honor of Wolfe Kelman,* New York, 1978.

Display Typography by Guenet Abraham

Library of Congress Cataloging-in-Publication Data
Peli, Pinchas.
[Shabbat shalom]
The Jewish sabbath: a renewed encounter/Peli, Pinchas H.
p. cm.
Reprint. Previously published: Shabbat shalom.
Washington, D.C.: B'nai B'rith Books, © 1988.
1. Sabbath—Meditations. I. Title.
BM685.P36 1991
296.4'1—dc20 91-52847
ISBN 0-8052-0998-0 (pbk.)

Manufactured in the United States of America

Schocken Books 1991 Edition

A bar and bat mitzvah present
for our grandchildren
Mordekhai Avishar and Margalit Har-shefi
Shimon Tzvi and Hila Elon
Joshua *1:8;* Isaiah *59:21*

Contents

Preface

Everyone carries, within, a special image of the Sabbath. Tell me what your Sabbath is like, and I will tell you who you are and what kind of a person you are. While your Sabbath is strictly personal, singular and unique, it nevertheless portrays a mosaic of components absorbed while you are carried over the waves of life.

Environmental influences, people, ideas, events and melodies blend together to impact on our Sabbath. When looking into our own renewed encounter with the Sabbath, we are directed toward confronting and acknowledging the various ingredients of which it is composed.

It is, I believe, inconceivable to discuss or write about Judaism without allotting the Sabbath a central place – as indeed nearly every great Jewish teacher and thinker in every generation has done. With all this, not one of them can claim to have laid down the final definitive word about the Sabbath in a purely "objective" and detached manner.

The Sabbath is so integral a part of the life of

every Jew that the ancient rabbis state that "the Sabbath outweighs all other commandments."[1] They base this statement on the words of the prophet who equates one who refrains from profaning the Sabbath to one who keeps away from all evil.[2] They emphasize that the same idea is found not only in the Prophets but also in the other parts of Scriptures.

The great medieval philosopher and codifier, Moses Maimonides, postulates in his Code of Law[3] that a Jew who transgresses all the Laws of the Torah is still considered a Jew, albeit a sinful one; but one who desecrates the Sabbath can no longer be considered a Jew. The Sabbath is thus the last trait of one's Jewishness and it is hard, if not utterly impossible, to conceive of the Jewish people without the Sabbath. None other than Achad Ha'am, the famed modern "nonreligious" Jewish philosopher, formulated the oft-quoted saying: *"More than Israel kept the Sabbath, it is the Sabbath which kept Israel.*[4]

Writing about the Sabbath, one must delve into all the sources of Judaism – historical, legal, philosophical, and literary. This has been done in the following chapters. The possibility existed for dividing the materials in a chronological or typological manner, i.e., the Sabbath in the Bible, in Rabbinic literature, in Jewish philosophy, etc. – a method which has been used in many anthologies on the Sabbath. Instead, our approach to the Sabbath has been as to an organic, growing entity of actual Jewish life;

an entity in the making from the earliest Biblical times to the present.

The words in Exodus, *"And the children of Israel shall observe the Sabbath to make the Sabbath,"*[5] are an integral part of the very nature of the Sabbath. Every generation "makes" the Sabbath again and again, and so, I believe, must ours.

These chapters may easily be used for Bible study groups, as in the course of their unfolding the story of the Sabbath, they touch in depth on nearly every Biblical text that deals with the Sabbath. In addition, to make these texts readily available, they are presented in Appendix A at the end of this book. The twenty-three chapters of the body of the book follow an inner rhythm. They attempt to represent the quintessence of a tremendously prolific literature on the Sabbath in Jewish tradition, as captured in the grasp of one person. They also draw heavily upon subjective, and undeniably personal, resources.

While this work was meant as an impassionate study of some classical Jewish sources and an attempt at a contemporary understanding of the Sabbath, it could not escape the author's indebtedness to many personal factors which enter into the final presentation.

It would be impossible to catalogue them all; it would, however, be equally impossible not to mention some of them as we present the following chapters.

A powerful example is the effect of growing up

in Jerusalem, where the Sabbath is almost a physical reality to be experienced with all of one's senses. The writer cannot overlook this autobiographical fact which enabled him to experience the simultaneous unfolding of all three dimensions of the Sacred: Time, Space and the Person (see the fifth chapter, "Three Dimensions of Existence"). The Sabbath – sacred time, Jerusalem – sacred space, and a community of men and women who have truly striven to represent the third dimension of the sacred – the dimension of the Jew whose life is illuminated all week long by Sabbath's radiant light.

This childhood environment thus provided a poignant living commentary to the Biblical text in Leviticus, where the observance of the Sabbath is ordained one time after the other, each time in another setting. First *"Each person should fear his mother and father and observe My Sabbaths;"* and then again, *"Observe My Sabbaths and fear my sanctuaries."*[6] The observance of the Sabbath as sacred time is thus placed in between the other two dimensions of the Sacred, that of sacred space ("My sanctuaries") and that of the mystery of one's personal origin ("his mother and father").

Celebrating the Sabbath in Jerusalem with ancestors for whom the day was a beloved and longed-for friend is no doubt reflected in this renewed encounter with the Sabbath. This is gratefully acknowledged, even as it is shared with those who were not privileged to experience the same biographical circumstance.

The motivation for sharing the Sabbath with others prompted my wife Penina and me to open our home ever so often to host friends of various religious or non-religious convictions, to share our Sabbath with them. As we wished to expand this home hospitality, a new institution was created some fifteen years ago, now well known as *Shabbat Yachad*, "Sabbath of Togetherness," where hundreds of families have the opportunity to get together for a communal celebration of the Sabbath in joy, study and genuine fellowship. This kind of Sabbath retreat, with its dual emphasis on both the Sabbath and togetherness, is a kind of pilot program which could, and hopefully will, be emulated in Jewish communities the world over (see Appendix Three), as it has been already in many circles in Israel. In addition, the "togetherness" of *Shabbat Yachad* has produced a strong bond with one of the most distinguished Jewish communities in the Diaspora – Congregation Shaar Hashomayim in Montreal, Canada – and with its spiritual leader, Rabbi Wilfred Zeev Shuchat, a loyal friend and active partner in this unique Sabbath project.

The experience of *Shabbat Yachad*, its participants and teachers, ably orchestrated by its program director Penina Peli, is reflected in the following pages and is acknowledged with deep gratitude.

Numerous books and articles on the Sabbath were consulted in the writing of these chapters. Mostly, I drew on those articles and books which to me were not just "bibliography" items, but also "spoke" to me in a very personal way. I was amazed to find how precious the Sabbath was to my great and beloved teachers and to many of my best friends, discovering that the greater part of any objectively-selected bibliography on the subject would be made up of works penned by personal friends. How good it is to know that one's teachers and friends along the way are also "soul brothers" in the realm of the Sabbath. Of my teachers, let me mention the two who more than any others molded my thoughts and actions. They are my revered father, the Jerusalem-born Rabbi Mordechai Ha-Cohen of blessed memory, who for ten full years edited and published single-handedly a biweekly periodical named *Neroth Shabbat* (Sabbath Lights), devoted solely to the Sabbath, and my late teacher who, in the last years of his life, was almost as close to me as my father – Rabbi Abraham Joshua Heschel. His book – *The Sabbath: Its Meaning for Modern Man* – remains a classic lighthouse to all who wish to truly experience the Sabbath. Thirty-five years after its publication there is room, however, for a "renewed encounter."

My distinguished brother Rabbi Shmuel Avidor Hacohen has contributed greatly to bringing the Sabbath experience to hundreds of thousands of homes all over Israel through his inimitable television program Ba'ah Shabbat (Sabbath is Here).

Among those dear friends and scholars whose writing on the Sabbath enriched my own thinking I would like to mention Dayan Israel Grunfeld and Rabbi Hayim Halevy Donin of blessed memory and יבלח"ט Professors Rabbi Joseph B. Soloveitchik, Andre Neher, Emil Fackenheim, Norman Lamm, Samuel H. Dresner, Emanuel Rackman, Wolfe Kelman, Walter Wurzburger, Irving Greenberg and Marshall T. Meyer. Their books and articles on the Sabbath, and in particular their personal friendship, are an inspiration in bringing the light of Sabbath into our life.

Acknowledgement of thanks go to Ms. Dahlia Gottan, head of world Wizo education department and her colleagues, Ms. Sally Horowitz and Heddie Hoffman, who initiated this book as part of a series of Wizo World Bible Day publications; to my beloved son Avraham Deuel (Dudie) Peli, and to Ms. Barbara Blechner Sevde for valuable editorial advice and help; to Seymour Rossel, gifted author and editor for his special interest in this and my other works; Dr. Michael Neiditch and Betty Fishman, my friends at B'nai Brith Books; and, last but not least, to my wife and life's companion and collaborator, Penina.

The Jewish Sabbath

All of Judaism in One Word

If we were to condense all of Judaism – its faith, thought, life, poetry and dreams – into a single word, there is but one word which could be used – *Shabbat*, or as it is referred to in English, the "Sabbath."[7]

There are hardly any words of endearment and adoration which have not been applied over the generations to describe the Sabbath, and yet its full impact and meaning are inexhaustible. As the Sabbath itself returns to us anew every week, fresh and radiant, sparkling and enchanting – so, too, understanding of the Sabbath takes on new meaning, new heights and new depths, as we continually study and probe the vast recesses of creativeness sparked and generated by this one word: Sabbath.

Foremost is, of course, the Hebrew Bible – where the Sabbath first emerged in its divine majesty and where it gradually unfolds in its colorful human vision of dignity and delight. Every aspect of the Sabbath as it grew and flowered in the course of many generations in the minds, hearts, and souls of countless sages, poets, and plain folk, has its foundation in the Bible. Here, the mysterious and boundless well is bubbling over with the living waters on which the Sabbath thrives to this day. It is to the pages of the Bible that we always turn to meet the essence of the Sabbath. Everything that was added in the course of many generations to make the Sabbath the splendid and complex treasure it is today would have little meaning, were it not for the image of the Sabbath given to us in the Hebrew Bible. In our present attempt for a contemporary renewed encounter with the Sabbath, it is necessary to turn from time to time to these expressions of the Sabbath's essence in the Bible.

Mountains on a Thin Thread

Although the Sabbath is generally held to be one of the major foundations of Biblical religion – and of Judaism as a way of life – the actual number of verses dealing with the Sabbath in the Bible is rather small.[8]

Already in the Mishnah (ed. cir. 200 CE) the *Tanna*[9] states that the ratio of oral traditions and actual practices regarding the Sabbath heavily outweighed the scriptural traditions on which they are based.[10] They are aptly described by the Mishnah as "mountains hanging on a thin thread." Indeed, the creative output concerning the Sabbath has risen to tall and heavy "mountains"; the biblical "thread" on which they hang is, however, strong enough to hold them up high. Sabbath in the Bible is in no way just "one more" commandment ordained or "one more" idea promulgated. It represents, rather, the very essence of the biblical message – Scripture's basic understanding of God,

World and Humanity, and their mutual interaction. It is, in more than one way, the meaning-giving component of human existence.

The Sabbath as first encountered in the Bible[11] does not make its entrance as a single isolated event, but as the very culmination of the whole story of creation, the gate through which we are ushered into the world.

From this vantage point, the Sabbath is, like the Bible itself, not merely a "Jewish" entity. While it partakes of an added "particularistic" dimension, it remains first and foremost universal. It offers the biblical and "Jewish" answer to questions which are not necessarily Jewish. They are the ultimate questions concerned with life and death, with the meaning (if it indeed possesses meaning) of the world; with human frailty versus the power of Nature and the glory of God; and other such intrinsically human questions.

In general, there are no "Jewish" questions as such in the Bible or in Judaic thought as a whole. The questions dealt with are always universal; the answers, Jewish.

Creation as Revelation

If the first chapters of Genesis are but another ancient creation legend or Near Eastern myth, then everything else in the Bible, the all-encompassing edifice of revelation and prophecy built on this foundation, might easily tumble.

Considering Higher and Lower Bible criticism for whatever they are worth (notwithstanding their often anti-Semitic motivations) and taking into account all the possible hypotheses of modern studies of comparative literature and religion, the present writer follows the school of thought (presently gaining more and more empirical ground and respectability) that sees in the biblical account of creation not necessarily a scientific account but a most unique and revolutionary approach, without which the entire biblical insight – regarding God, world, and humanity – has no foot to stand on. Take away the Genesis creation story and all of Ethical Monotheism is bunk; the eternal message of redemption and salvation, fairy tales.

The Sabbath comes to confirm and affirm the

biblical story of Creation. It stands as a constant, living and ever-renewed testimony to this story, which binds together "Heaven" and "Earth," which brings God into this world to be celebrated by humanity, and which consequently gives meaning, direction and hope to the world created and kept alive by God who trusts in His own handiwork. "A God of trust"[12] says the Rabbinic interpretation: "A God who manifests trust in His world and proceeds to create it."[13]

Sabbath is the day on which this trust is manifested. It is an ever-renewed testimony to the wonder of creation.

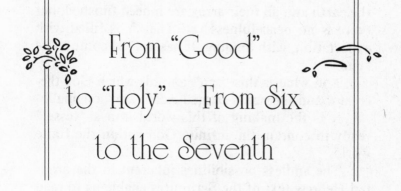

From "Good" to "Holy"—From Six to the Seventh

After six successive days of creation of the material world, a world seen as "good," even "very good,"[14] in the eyes of the Lord, comes the seventh day.

> And God saw all that He had made, and found it very good. And there was evening and there was morning, the sixth day. The heaven and the earth were finished, and all their array. On the seventh day God finished the work which He had been doing, and He ceased on the seventh day from all the work which he had done. And God blessed the seventh day and declared it holy, because on it God ceased from all the work of creation which He had done.[15]

The world created in the first six days is not, however, the end of creation. Following the six days of the creation of the material world, there is yet to come another day, a hallowed day – a day that brings the six days not only to an "end" (finish), but also to their "end" (destination).[16] The heaven and the earth and all their array are indeed finished, but there is no peacefulness yet. The air is filled with expectation, with longing. It has not yet come to its "end."

And what is this "end" towards which God-the-creator and the newly-created Adam are "longing"?

It is the making of this world into a "vessel" ready to contain the infinite God within the finite world.

The endless possibilities inherent in the original Hebrew text of the Scriptures enable us to read the verses concerning the Sabbath in the following way:

> The heaven and the earth and all their array were finished, had reached their destination, yet were still *longing.*[17] On the seventh day God *made* all the work which he had been doing into a vessel.[18] For in six days the Lord made heaven and earth. On the seventh He abstained from work and breathed a soul into it.[19]

The Sabbath was the breath of the spirit of God breathed into the mammoth body of the created world of nature. On the Sabbath, the world of matter obtained a soul.[20]

Here we are confronted with the great biblical revolution of breaking away from the cobweb of magic and from the shackles of dread into a new, unique and different, bright and redeeming realm of the Sacred.

The world in itself is not holy. Nature is desacralized in the Bible.[21] Only God and humanity made in His image are able to make it holy. To the dimension of the Good of the material world created in six days, and qualified to function in harmony, is now added a new dimension: the dimension of the spiritual, the seventh day.

Nature can be "good," even "very good," but it is not God. One must remember that it is God who, by His free will, created nature.

The human being created in the Image of God is part of the world of nature, created "to rule" it, not to be ruled by it. The human person is capable of transcending the material world, while being in it and with it. To prove this, there is a "holy" (i.e., "special") day, hallowed by God.

As God concluded His work on the material world and put humanity into it at the conclusion of the sixth day, He added a seventh day, a special day which He set aside in order to encounter humanity so they might celebrate together the birth of a new, brave world. It is the Sabbath that marks the point of "togetherness" of God and humanity. It takes place in the moment in which God re-enters the created world, in biblical language, on the day which "He sanctified," that is to say, on the day in which the Holy One made His sacred presence felt.

An interesting idea is taught by the Maharal (Rabbi Judah Loew, 1520-1609) of Prague: everything in the material world has six dimensions, or directions (East, West, North, South, up, and down), and can be weighed and measured. The six dimensions are the extent of the realm of matter created in six days. The Sabbath adds to the world a seventh dimension, the dimension of the Holy, which gives meaning to the other six.

Although things belonging to the seventh dimension cannot be tested in the same way as material things, nor can they be weighed and measured, their presence is unquestionable. Can love, trust, faithfulness, and their like be measured or weighed? Yet, can their existence be denied?

Now it is for humanity, sharing this seventh dimension with God, to respond to the challenge of the Holy, to receive and accept the Godly presence without abandoning his earthly "here-and-now"-ness. The Sabbath comes to make this possible. As God rested, desisted from all other work in order to hallow, to sanctify, so humanity is told to desist from all work, in order to sanctify, to hallow, to encounter God, the Holy One.

> Remember the Sabbath day, to keep it holy. Six days you shall labor, and do all your work; but the seventh day is a Sabbath unto the Lord your God; in it you shall not do any work, you, or your son, or your daughter, your manservant, or your maidservant, or your cattle, or the sojourner who is within your gates; for in the six days the Lord made heaven and earth, the sea and all that is in them, and rested on the seventh day; therefore the Lord blessed the Sabbath day and hallowed it.[22]

The Sabbath is a crucible in time where humanity in its limited creatureliness and God in His enormous creatorliness meet each other halfway to celebrate holiness in time.

If we may portray it graphically, it would look something like this:

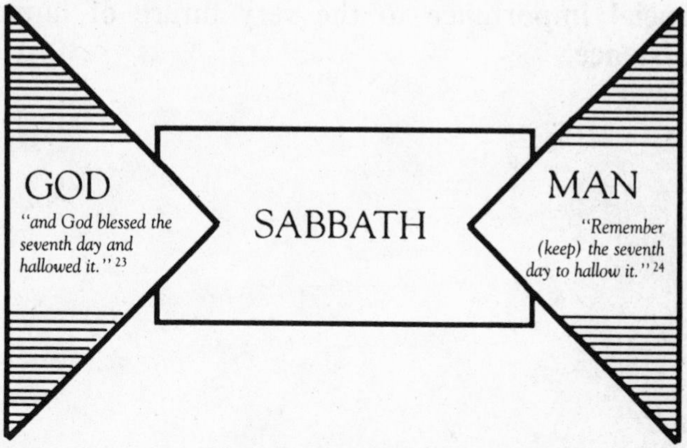
GOD
"and God blessed the seventh day and hallowed it." 23
SABBATH
MAN
"Remember (keep) the seventh day to hallow it." 24

What brings God and humanity together is the mutual act of hallowing. The well-known Hebrew expression *Shabbat Kodesh*, should not be translated as it usually is – "Holy Sabbath"[25] – but rather "Sabbath of Holiness." Remembering or keeping the Sabbath in manifold ways, as we shall see, has only one purpose: to hallow it. Not observing the Sabbath is described in the Bible as "profaning" or "desecrating" it,[26] an expression applied to non-observance of Sabbath even in modern Hebrew to this day.

What do we mean by "holiness"? How does a modern human being grasp or even sense the sacred? Why is it needed at all?

The Sabbath, growing and developing out of the bedrock of the biblical concept of sacredness, may have some of the answers to these questions – answers which, in the long run, may be of vital and crucial importance to the very future of human existence.

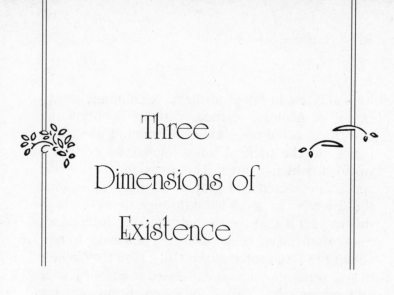

Three Dimensions of Existence

A world without the dimension of the sacred is a world without meaning, without direction, without purpose.

The physical world of nature may be "good" in the sense of efficiency, it may constitute a good machine that works well and thus fulfills the expectations of its maker; it is not "good" in the sense that it is not evil. Physical energy does not know how to differentiate between the ethical and the non-ethical, between bestowing life and blessing or wreaking havoc and disaster.

Moreover, until humanity managed to "set aside" (this is perhaps the original meaning of the verb *kds*[27]), to hallow, to declare sacred or "special," certain "pieces" of time and space, both time and space seemed endless, non-distinguishable, impossible to grasp at all. A line had to be drawn between special, sacred time and mundane, profane time, between sacred space and ordinary space, before humanity could relate to them. Astronomy, topography, or geology, sciences without intentionality and ritual, could not,without religion on its various levels, do the trick of adjusting humanity to the world in which it lives. This division of time and space into sacred and profane is much older than the Bible.[28] The great breakthrough of the Bible in this respect is that the Sacred was freed from blind, magical, primeval religious forces and came to represent the One source of the Holy, God the Creator of All, whose holiness is expressed in acts of justice and compassion. This is reflected throughout the Bible. The holiness of the Holy One as revealed in the Bible also serves as an example for human beings to emulate: "You shall be holy – because I your Lord am Holy"[29] is the cornerstone of the entire Bible, the whole Bible in miniature.[30]

There are three dimensions of the Holy, i.e., where the presence of the Holy One can be encountered within the reality of this mundane world. They are the dimensions of time, space and person. These three dimensions which define reality are stated in an ancient mystical Hebrew book[31] as *olam* ("cosmos" = space), *shanah* ("year" = time cycle), and *nefesh* ("soul" = person). No reality in the here-and-now could be completely grasped without all three elements present.

Take for instance the table supporting the paper on which these lines are written. It exists in space, it takes some time for us to see it – and if we are not here to see it, it would not exist for us at all.

The biblical created world emerges as a world of time and space. "And God said, Let us make a human, in Our image, after Our likeness" – humanity the person that testifies to the existence of this world. "In the beginning" – time, "God created heaven and earth" – space. While given dominion to rule the world and subdue it, humanity could easily "lose" its unique, "special," in-the-image-of-God personality, even while fulfilling its role. While taming Mother Nature, we are likely to lose sight of our Father in heaven. The human, that of all beings was endowed with the divine "image of God," may easily forfeit freedom since its task to fill the world is never ending – twenty-four hours a day, seven days a week. The ingenious and intricate tools that we make to control nature require constant and uninterrupted attention. The fight between our limited life-span time and the enormous space surrounding us, the constant tension between time and space, may easily destroy us. Our time is always shared by others. There is no private ownership of time. When a person's "time" comes no treasure in the world can buy more. The being who conquers space is over-ruled by time. Time takes us in a non-stop procession towards death; a moment gone is a moment dead, we will never see it again. Time becomes our enemy. It joins forces with space, the "cursed" earth, that brings forth "thorns and thistles," and demands constantly "the sweat of his brow."[32]

Clutched in between the two squeezing prongs

of time and space, who can think of the dimension of dignified human existence, the dimension of the person, that which makes us "special," free and open to participate by choice in the spiritual as well as in the material adventure of our being?

Now that God the creator has set us free from the forces of nature and has appointed us master over them – can we also master our own nature? Can we realize in full the freedom that is ours? Or will we forever remain enslaved to the role of master that we play? As our ability extends to control volcanos on earth, to take off on the high seas, one contemporary thinker observed, will we also be able to control the volcano which is within us? To fare the high seas of spiritual potentials?

Enter: the Sabbath.

A Built-in Corrective

For many decades Christian (mainly German) Bible researchers made a consistent effort to steal the Bible from Israel, its legitimate heirs.

In part, they set out to "prove" that the Tanakh was not at all unique or original, but merely "one more" document from antiquity. The Sabbath, too, fell victim to these concepts. An elaborate literature grew around the findings that there was a day named Shappatu[33] in ancient Babylon, a day on which work was prohibited because of "bad luck." This day, which was marked out as a day of mourning, fell on the seventh, fourteenth, twenty-first and twenty-eighth of the month. What more did one need to "prove" the "origin" of the Hebrew Sabbath? The fact that the Sabbath is not tied in at all with the cycle of the moon, or for that matter with any cycle within nature, was deliberately overlooked; the fact that the whole idea of a seven-day week (now almost universally accepted) was not known until the Bible[34] and was in no way connected with created physical nature, but with the will of the metaphysical Creator, that too, was conveniently ignored together with the fact that the Babylonian *shappatu* is marked in ways (fasting, mourning, etc.) which have nothing in common with the Sabbath as we know it.

It was only recently that biblical scholarship, Jewish and non-Jewish alike, came to realize and affirm that the Sabbath is – in the words of John L. McKenzie: "a peculiarly Israelite institution with no parallel... it is a novel concept of sacred time... nothing like it known elsewhere."[35] McKenzie sees the originality of the Sabbath also in the way it is manifested in practice: "abstention from profane work and the consecration of time by not using it... The Sabbath may easily be included among the earliest and the distinctly Israelite convenant institutions."[36] Martin Buber, following a long line of renowned scholars, has this to say: "In Israel, and as far as we know, in Israel only, the seven-day week developed as the ever-returning passage from toil to appeasement and from discord to harmony."[37]

The Sabbath, if understood properly, could not conceivably come into being anywhere outside the sphere of the Hebrew Bible and the global message of Judaism. It developed, of course, over may generations and took on layers of lore and law, but it will always remain the "peculiar treasure" of the Jewish people, a reflection of its own conception of God's world and of humanity's share in it. The Sabbath stands as a living witness for the covenantal partnership between God and the people of Israel:

> You shall keep My Sabbaths, for this is a sign between Me and you throughout the ages that you may know that I am the Lord who sanctifies you. You shall keep the Sabbath, for it is holy for you... Six days may work be done, but on the seventh day there shall be a Sabbath of complete rest, holy to the Lord... The children of Israel shall keep the Sabbath observing the Sabbath throughout the ages as a covenant for all time: it shall be a sign forever between Me and the people of Israel. For in six days the Lord made heaven and earth and on the seventh day He ceased from work and was refreshed.[38]

Even before the world was created, says an old Midrash,[39] there were seven things which entered God's thoughts as prerequisite for creation. Among these is the Sabbath. It is not that after working for six days, God, or for that matter, humanity, tires and needs rest. The Sabbath was built into the scheme of creation even before the work of creation began. In the words of the liturgist, the Sabbath is "Last in creation, first in intention,"[40] "the very purpose of the works of Heaven and Earth."[41]

What would the world have been like, had it not been for the built-in corrective to its ills and woes called Sabbath? What would the world have been like if creation had gone on and on without an "end," without rest, without renewal, without delight, without holiness?

The Author's Signature

The Sabbath stands at the end of the story of creation. As the Creator finished His works, He looked back to review it and saw "that all He had made" was "very good." Not that every detail, by itself, was actually "very good," but the sum total of it was.[42]

As is the wish of the artist, He too wanted to sign His name on His work of art, the world, before handing it over to humanity to master and use. Thus the last two words in the first chapter of Genesis are *Yom Hashishi* ("and it was evening and it was morning the sixth day"). The first two words in the second chapter are *Wa-yekhulu Hashomayim* ("the heaven and earth were finished"). When the two chapters are joined together (as it is done in the recital of the Sabbath *kiddush*), the two last words of Chapter One and the first two words of Chapter Two yield the four-letter name of God, Y-H-W-H, the acronym representing as it were the signature of the Author of the World.[43]

In this case, however, unlike most artists, God

the artist did not step away from His masterpiece after handing it over to its new owners. The God of the Bible is not Aristotle's unmoved mover. He is moved and moves along, with the work of art He created.

Furthermore, the work of creation, it is true, was finished in six days; the "finishing touch," however, did not take place on the sixth day, but on the seventh.

Thus we read "The Heavens were finished [on the sixth day], and all their array; And on the seventh day God finished the work which he had been doing."[44] From this verse it is not clear when the "finishing" occurred – was it on the sixth or on the seventh? It seems that the real "finishing" did not occur until the seventh day, which marks the real completion of creation.

The Sabbath stands at the crossroads between two distinct phases of creation, at the junction between nature and history. "The heaven and earth were *finished*," say the Rabbis, "the work of the righteous and the wicked began."[45] Even after finishing the creation of heaven and earth, God's job was not over. He remained very much involved in His creative work of art. Many troubles loomed ahead to upset this world of His. It was still going to make him "sad at his heart" and He was going to "regret the fact that He made [it]."[46] True, but "in time of joy – rejoice."[47] Now it was time to rejoice and celebrate the newly-born world. The Sabbath will thus remain, now and forever, the "birthday celebration" of the world, the ongoing ceremony of its dedication.[48]

At the end of every day of creation it says: "And there was evening and there was morning." Only the seventh day is not given natural parameters of evening and morning. Why? Because the Sabbath is a day that belongs to eternity. It is a gift from eternity to our temporal existence. It is, according to the Rabbis of the Midrash[49] the day to which the prophet Zechariah refers when he says that "there shall be a continuous day – only the Lord knows when – of neither day nor night and there shall be light at eventide."[50]

> ...And God blessed the seventh day and hallowed it, because on it He ceased from all the work which He created *la-asot.*[51]

La-asot is the last word which concludes the original Hebrew biblical story of creation. It is translated "created and made" (King James) or "which He had done" (New JPS). Some rabbinic interpretations render the word *la-asot* in a most simple, yet very instructive way: "to do," or "to be made." The verse is thus to be read in the following manner: "And God blessed the seventh day and made it holy because on it God ceased all the work which [God] created [for humanity] to do," or " to continue doing." It was on the Sabbath that the world was dedicated and handed over to man. Creation *ex-nihilo*, out of nothing, was finished. This only God could do. Now human beings must use all the "very good" materials and energies created by

God "to make" this world, which is still incomplete, waiting for humanity to finish it.[52]

A partnership is thus formed between God and humanity. They are joined in a common bond and purpose, "to do" and to make this world into a world in the center of which stands the Sabbath, which itself has now to be made, shaped, and filled with holiness.

A World to Come

Sabbath is not a "weekend." It is in the center of being, joining together nature and history. It is also in the center of the life of the individual Jew and of Judaism.

When Franz Rosenzweig came to sum up the essence of Judaism, he formulated it around three highlights: Creation, Revelation and Redemption.[53] These interrelate with each other and interact with the three components of reality as the Bible conceives them: God, world and humanity. Each one of these components relates to the other two but is not identical to either. World is not God (as in Pantheism) but God's creation; God is not humanity (as in Christianity); humanity is not world (as in Buddhism). Judaism sees the three as separate entities, interacting meaningfully as they all take part in a structured but dynamic cosmic drama that has a beginning (creation), a middle (revelation) and an end (redemption). Rosenzweig ingeniously attached his philosophy to the popular Jewish symbol known as the Star of David which consists of two triangles superimposed on each other.[54] Thus, following Rosenzweig, the first triangle is that of Reality and it consists of God, world, humanity (Figure 1); the second, that of Meaning, consisting of Creation, Revelation and Redemption (Figure 2). When imposed on each other (Figure 3) they represent Judaism in its totality.

Fig. 1
Reality

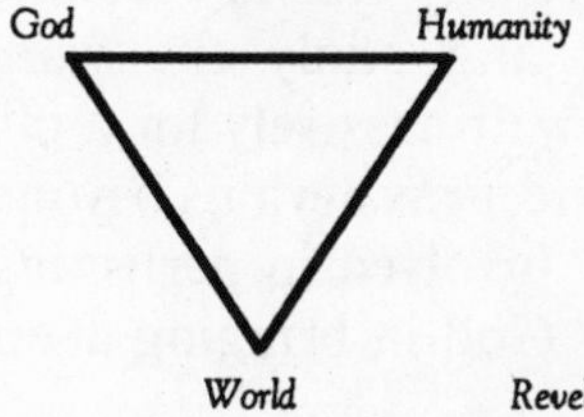

Fig. 2
Meaning

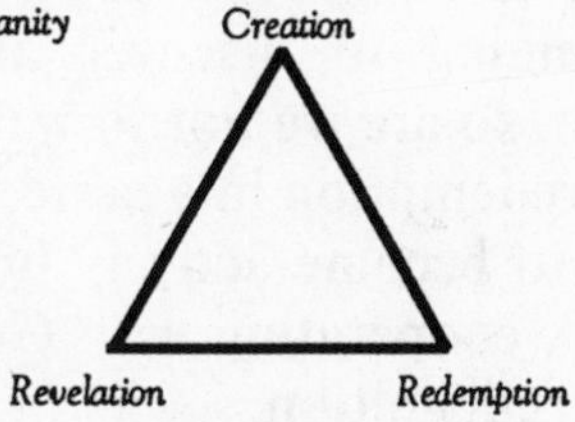

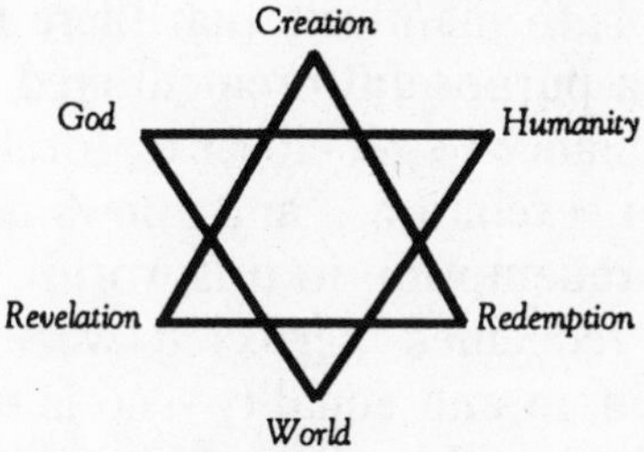

Fig. 3
Star of Redemption

The Sabbath stands out as a remarkable meeting point of all three elements representing meaning. Its source is a remembrance of Creation, its observance the only "word" relating to ritual in the Ten Words of Revelation at Sinai, and finally it is very often referred to as a "foretaste of the world to come," the world of Redemption.

The world to come which we are talking about is not eschatological, hidden beyond history or life, but can be made to come alive every Sabbath. As we are expected to become partners with God in creation, by continuing to develop and advance this world in all spheres of reality and in revelation by continuing to discover and study the words of Torah, so are we not to wait passively for a miraculous redemption in a perfect mysterious beyond, but have to become actively involved in perfecting this world, cooperating with God in bringing about the final redemption.

The Sabbath reassures us that this is possible.

The Sabbath manifests that there is an end to creation, as a purposeful premeditated act of God; it gives us a chance to get closer to Torah – the main depository of revelation – and allows us to taste of the fruits of redemption in this world.

As the redeemed perfected world will be a world of freedom and equality – so is the Sabbath; as the redeemed world will be harmonious, will have no struggle between classes of rich and poor, no clashes between humanity and nature – so the Sabbath is meant to be a harmonious and peaceful day when all strife, competitiveness and envy are blotted out, when no financial or other kind of worry is permitted.

The Sabbath is thus both "the end of the beginning" and "the beginning of the end," a well-spring of trust and hope for a better, perfected world.

A strong sense of this is expressed in the Sabbath liturgy, as for instance, in the grace after meals on the Sabbath we say "May the Merciful One grant us a day that is wholly Sabbath and rest – the life of the world to come." The three Amida services for the Sabbath, evening, morning, and afternoon, point as well to the three elements suggested by Rosenzweig. The theme of the biblical passage quoted in the Amida on Friday night points to creation.[55] The theme of the Sabbath morning service deals with revelation ("May Moses rejoice in the gift he received"), while the afternoon Minha service pronounces redemption ("You are one and your name One").[56]

If eternity means the combined simultaneous experience of all three tenses of time – past, present, and future – then by celebrating the Sabbath we are able to experience eternity every week. We find ourselves in accord with the heartbeat of all time, as conceived in the Judaic vision of the universe.

The Five "M"s

We first encounter the Sabbath as she steps out of the mist and the myth of creation.

In the book of Genesis there is no mention of the Sabbath as it relates to human beings. All we hear is that God rested on the seventh day, that He blessed the seventh day, that He sanctified it. Only in the second book of the Pentateuch, in Exodus, do we meet the Sabbath again, this time turning to us. She does not, however, confront us directly as yet; her face is still veiled in mystery. She is still the Sabbath of the Lord, part of His mysterious works.

The children of Israel, stranded in the desert, are marveling at the strange sight of food being showered down to them from heaven. They wonder and ask in astonishment: *Man-hu*, "What is it?" Their amazed query remains forever the name of this marvelous food: *man-na.*

They go out into the field every morning and gather it, an exact ration for each person. Comes Friday, the day before the Sabbath, and suddenly, wonder upon wonder, the heavens shower for each a double portion. They rush to inform Moses.

> And he said unto them, this is that which the Lord hath spoken. Tomorrow is a solemn rest, a holy Sabbath unto the Lord; bake that which ye shall bake, and seethe that which ye will seethe; and all that remaineth over, lay up for you to be kept until the morning...And Moses said, Eat that today, for today is a Sabbath unto the Lord. Today ye shall not find in the field... Six days ye shall gather it, but on the seventh day is the Sabbath, in it there shall be none.[57]

The Sabbath comes to us here as if it were built into the mystery of creation itself.

"That there was a double portion on the sixth day, but none on the seventh," says Martin Buber, "indicates that the Sabbath does not exist exclusively in the world of human beings, it also functions outside their world."[58] The truth is that here, for the first time, the Sabbath relates to human beings.

If God wills, there is a world. Willed by God, nature takes its course; willed by God, nature changes its course. If He wills, bread comes down from heaven as it comes up from the earth; but never on the Sabbath. True, it is His Sabbath – but it is meant for us, too! All laws concerning the preparation of food for the Sabbath prior to the onset of Sabbath itself, which are practiced by observant Jews to this very day, are learned from the mysterious event of the manna and its "observance" of the Sabbath.

The Sabbath, however, does not remain in the realms of myth and mystery alone. With the consolidation of the tribes of Israel as a people, the Sabbath moves on to become institutionalized as part of a religious-national constitution. It appears now as a basic *mitzvah*, as one of the foundations of the life of the people.

We are approaching now what came to be considered the central event in the history of Israel and its religion: revelation at Sinai, the acceptance of the Ten Commandments. The major place which the Sabbath occupies in this event, the fact that it is the only ritual commandment to be thus documented, shows us how essential it was considered. Without abandoning its mythical and mystical beginnings, it moved to a new plane, to *mitzvah*, a "commandment," a Law which shows the way, which is the way.

Even now it will not become an arid lifeless law and will always be nourished on the one hand by the fascinating myth and mystery that preceded it, as well as by new insights of memory and meaning that will still be attached to it; the memory of the passage from slavery to freedom and the meaning of the combination of rest and holiness as it has been enacted in Jewish civilization throughout the ages.

Thus, if one wants to see the Sabbath in its full stature, one ought to follow her keeping in mind the six M formula (common to the Sabbath and all biblical holidays). One can easily observe how the Sabbath grows from *Myth* and *Mystery* to *Mitzvah, Memory,* and *Meaning*, and from there to the final stage: the *Messianic.* With every move she retains also the earlier layers, which can be seen if we cut through the Sabbath vertically, in the same way that the various layers could be clearly seen in an archeological *tel.* The Sabbath in the Bible grows in front of our eyes as a living organism. It still grows in depth of meaning and insight even today.

One may also notice the interesting shift which takes place in the attribution of the Sabbath in the Bible. First, it is referred to only as "Sabbath unto the Lord,"[59] then, also, as "Sabbath unto you."[60] As humanity intensifies its partnership with God, humanity also enlarges its share in the Sabbath. In the beginning it is only He, God, who sanctifies the Sabbath;[61] afterwards: You, humanity, should sanctify.[62] It is on the sacred "ground" of the Sabbath that the partnership of God and humanity comes to full fruition. It is in this sanctuary-in-time that God and humanity join together in holiness.

"Thou Shalt Not!"

Even before the Sabbath enters the realm of Mitzvah as the fourth of the ten commandments, we are told, as a result of watching how God observed the Sabbath in regard to the manna, not to engage in certain activities, such as baking and cooking. We are also restricted in our movements on the Sabbath day.[63] It is, however, in the Ten Words (often referred to as the Ten Commandments) that we were ordered not "to do any work."

The prohibition of labor on the Sabbath is repeated in the Bible in different ways no less than twelve times. Included are: kindling of fire;[64] baking and cooking;[65] gathering wood;[66] moving out of a prescribed area;[67] plowing and harvesting;[68] carrying loads;[69] engaging in business;[70] buying and selling.[71]

In addition to the kinds of labor directly or indirectly mentioned in the Bible, an enormous body of "thou shall not's" were associated with the Sabbath in Rabbinic literature and are practiced today by many Jews.

While we are told that all work is forbidden on the Sabbath, states Rabbi Solomon Goldman in his illuminating *Guide to the Sabbath*,[72] we still do not know the definition of work. Is work, he asks, to engage in gainful employment? Then it would follow that the professional house-painter, for example, would be permitted to paint his own home on the Sabbath, and his Sabbath would be indistinguishable from his weekday. Is the amount of energy expended or the fatigue involved used as a measure? Then the Sabbath would vary according to the physique, skill, and stamina of the individual. Is it to be left to the individual to personally decide what is work? Then there would be almost as many varieties of the Sabbath as there are Jews, because what is work for one may be pleasure for another.

The early Rabbis, by deducing from the various references of prohibited types of work mentioned in the Bible, formulated a comprehensive classification of the categories of labor forbidden on the Sabbath. They based their classification on the fact that the Sabbath commandment was repeated to Moses immediately after the full instructions were given to him for constructing the Tabernacle[73] and again by Moses to the Israelites immediately before he communicated those instructions. It is as if to say that however important, sacred, and urgent the task of building the Tabernacle is – it must not override the duty of refraining from work on the Sabbath. From this it follows that the tasks that were carried out in the construction of the Tabernacle are forbidden on the Sabbath. By an exhaustive analysis the Rabbis of the Mishnah classified the work which the construction of the Tabernacle involved under thiry-nine main categories (*avot melakhah*).

The thirty-nine types of work prohibited on the Sabbath as listed in the Mishnah are: 1) plowing, 2)sowing, 3) reaping, 4) sheaf-making, 5) threshing, 6) winnowing, 7) selecting, 8) grinding, 9) sifting, 10) kneading, 11) baking, 12) shearing, 13) bleaching, 14) combing raw materials, 15) dyeing, 16) spinning, 17, 18, 19) weaving processes, 20) separating into threads, 21) tying a knot, 22) untying a knot, 23) sewing, 24) tearing in order to sew, 25) trapping, 26) slaughtering, 27) skinning, 28, 29) tanning processes, 30) scraping hides, 31) cutting to shape, 32) writing, 33) erasing, 34) building, 35) demolishing, 36) extinguishing, 37) kindling a fire, 38) the final hammer blow, 39) carrying from one domain to another.[74]

The main categories, the *avot* or "ancestors," produced innumerable *toladot* or "offspring" which take up 174 chapters – the largest section on any subject – in the *Shulhan Arukh* (the *Code of Law*, edited in the 16th century) and fill a book of 400 pages composed by a contemporary Jerusalem Rabbi a few years ago.[75]

The word *melakhah* employed in the Hebrew Bible in connection with work on the Sabbath ("Six days thou shall work and do all your *melakhah* [work] but the seventh day is a Sabbath to the Lord thy God; in it thou shalt not do any *melakhah*") may give us the key to the common denominator of the various types of work forbidden on the Sabbath. Indeed, many distinguished Jewish thinkers have researched the matter and offered some illuminating explanations as to the "why" of the biblical prohibition of *melakhah* on the Sabbath. On one thing, however, all agree – the reason for resting on the Sabbath is not in order to work better during the week. Much dignity is given to work both in the Bible and in later Judaic thought, to the degree that one of the early Rabbis sees a positive commandment in the verse "Six days thou shalt work,"[76] thus considering idleness a sin. However, just as human beings do not live to eat but eat to live, so we do not rest to work, but vice versa, especially since rest is, as we saw and shall see further (see "Rest is a Created Thing") not just cessation from work, but an active verb. Why then the emphasis on not doing work on the Sabbath and the painstakingly meticulous effort to define forbidden work? If it is neither the physical effort nor the profit-making element that determines the nature of forbidden work, what then is it?

Why Not?

According to Philo,[77] the reason for not engaging in work on the Sabbath is primarily to free the people from any physical and manual occupation in order that they may concentrate their time and energy on spiritual and intellectual matters. The Sabbath is a day set aside for philosophizing, and nothing should disturb this activity.

A similar reason for the prohibition on working on the Sabbath is found in Rabbinic literature, expressed in its peculiar style:

> Said Torah: Lord of the Universe, when Israel enters the Land – what will happen to me? Said He [to Torah]: there is one mate that I give you – the day of Sabbath, when the Israelites are off from work and they enter the houses of worship and the houses of Study and deal with the Torah.[78]

Philo has yet another reason. He wrote in a society which was conveniently divided between masters who *never worked* and slaves who *never rested*, working twenty-four hours a day, seven days a week. He thus saw the Sabbath as a day that would revolutionize the set order; the slave would get a day of rest, the master would be forced to serve himself and learn the meaning of work. That would teach everyone that all human beings are essentially equal. To fully appreciate the meaning of this assertion, one has to recall Plato's and Aristotle's philosophical support of the contemporary scene, a scene dominated by a clear-cut division of human beings between slaves and masters.

Other reasons for the prohibition of work on the Sabbath are offered by modern Jewish thinkers. Samson Raphael Hirsch (1808-1888), asserts that God gave humanity the Sabbath day as an everlasting Covenant in order that humanity might understand that it is God who allows us mastery over the world. During the remainder of the week, humanity controls and subdues the earth for its own ends, but on the Sabbath, humanity must return it to God, mindful that the earth is "on loan" from God.

For Hirsch, to refrain from *melakhah* on the Sabbath means to refrain from acts which demonstrate human mastery over the earth, thereby recognizing and acknowledging that human mastery is a gift from God. It is therefore neither physical effort nor profit-making which determine what is considered "work," but any act "that shows humanity's mastery over the world by constructive exercise of his intelligence and skill." On the Sabbath humanity must refrain from God-like acts – creating new things, changing things from one state of being to another, etc.

With the Sabbath begins the transformation of humanity, says Hirsch.[79] We look upon nature and history, God and humanity, ourselves and our relation to Nature and to God and to other creatures with different eyes.

We do not crawl or tremble before Nature, we do not bend our knees; the name of God has made us free, free from the terrors of nature's forces; our covenant with God uplifts our souls above all nature's domain. "In heaven [we have] but Him, and beside Him [we need] nothing on earth!" We do not lord it over nature. The name of God has made us humble. Notwithstanding all the power with which we rule nature, we humbly bow our heads before the one most high Creator and Master, and desire to use the strength granted to us only in the service of God who has placed us in nature's garden, "to protect and to perfect it!" We do not crawl and tremble before the temporal power of human beings. The name of God has made us free, free from the fear of the many, and the worship of humanity. God is as near to the humble cottage as He is to the most magnificent mansion; the souls of His children in the meanest cradle are of as much account as the descendants of kings bedecked in silk. God is as near to those of quiet, humble calling as He is to the much acclaimed hero or heroine – and if God is with us in our quiet, honest labor, what can mere humans do to us? We have no enemy in the human family. The name of God has made us free, free from envy and arrogance, from hatred and enmity, from revenge and violence. Just as we feel ourselves bound up with God, so we see God's name stamped upon every one of our brothers and sisters. Hence this name draws everyone near to us, as our own kin, and teaches us to regard everyone's sphere as a place hallowed by divine dispensation. We do not look disdainfully upon the poorest among us, nor envy the richest. We grudge blessing to no one, a share of possessions to no one, pleasures and honors – or anything which God has conferred. "He who gathers much has in His eyes no more, he who gathers little has in His eyes no less than the measure allotted by God to each person."[80]

Issur melakhah – "abstinence from work," this is the sign which your God expects from you on every Sabbath. Abstinence from work is the sign which He seeks to prove whether you can still call yourself His. Abstinence from work is the sign by which you are to demonstrate that God is the Creator of heaven and earth, that He is also your Creator and that you, too, belong to Him.

For six days the world belongs to you, for six days you may exercise your dominion over everything that your God has created, and perform "melakhah;" you may stamp your creative impression upon everything and make it the agent of your will, the executor of your purpose. But on the seventh day you shall testify that, after all, the world is not yours, that you are not its ultimate ruler, but merely God's vassal on earth, that you live and work only by God's grace, that He is your Lord and

Master, the Lord and Master of the smallest as of the greatest creature within your ken. To this you shall testify by giving the world its freedom on this day, by retiring into that sphere which is subject to you and by not exerting your powers on any work of God to bend it to your purpose.

By *issur melakhah*, by abstinence from work on the Sabbath, you place yourself and your work reverently on God's holy altar.

By *issur melakhah* you make the twenty-four hours of the Sabbath a continual dedication of the world to your God and a consecration of yourself.

The bird, the fish, the animal that you refrain from catching on the Sabbath, the plant that you refrain from tearing up, the material that you refrain from fashioning or chiseling, or cutting or mixing, or molding, or preparing, all this inaction is but a demonstration of homage to your God, proclaiming Him Creator and Master and Lord of the world; and the child who refrains from catching the butterfly or plucking the blossom on the Sabbath glorifies the Almighty.

Abraham Joshua Heschel (1907-1972), the thinker who did more than anyone else to enhance the relevance of the Sabbath in modern times, sees in the abstention from work, any work, on the Sabbath, a way of achieving freedom in a world becoming more and more enslaved to dehumanizing technology. "We have fallen victims to the work of our hands; it is as if the forces we had conquered have conquered us....The Sabbath is the day on which we learn the act of surpassing civilization....The solution of mankind's most vexing problem will not be found in renouncing technical civilization, but in attaining some degree of independence from it.... On the Sabbath we live, as it were, independent of technical civilization."

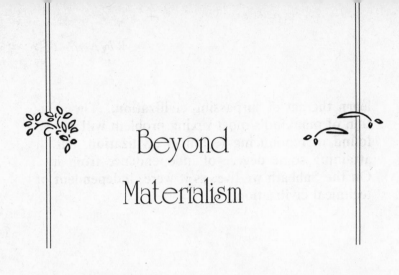

Beyond Materialism

If the Sabbath makes us sense the perfect and peaceful redeemed world-to-come, here is another reason for not engaging in work, especially business activities, on the Sabbath. A world in which there is business competition and a ruthless rat race to success is not the peaceful world of redemption.

One should not even handle money on the Sabbath because of *muktzeh.*[81] The world-to-come of which the Sabbath is a foretaste is a world without strife, without class struggle, without jealousy by those who have-not of those who have. Such a world is surely a world far removed from money, money-making, and what comes with it.

That is perhaps why the prophet Amos is so vehement in his condemnation of those who want "to swallow up the needy and destroy the poor," who wait impatiently for the Sabbath to go by, so that they may

> set forth wheat, making the *efa* [a measure of grain] small and the *shekel* great and falsifying the bal-

ances of deceit, that we may buy the poor for silver and the needy for a pair of shoes and sell the refuse of the wheat.[82]

At least as long as the Sabbath prevails, all these deceits could not be perpetrated.

They wait impatiently for the Sabbath to go by, in order to start their cheating and deceit. Those who cannot stand the Sabbath are the same people who cheat and deceive. Sabbath stands out as a constant protest against a world which forgot the essential difference between the "value" and the "price" of things; a world in which, when talking about the "value" of people, one thinks of how much money they have ("How much is he worth?"), a world in which possessions are put above the person.

As the Sabbath stands outside time, in a way it also stands outside and above financial restrictions which sometimes limit us in an oppressive way. In the past, it was not unusual among poor Jews to deprive themselves all week long in order to save and be able to "live it up" on the Sabbath. Even the poorest family would prepare the best for the Sabbath. When one prepares for his own family he thinks also of the needy wayfarer. A "guest for Sabbath" was an indispensable part of the Sabbath celebration in every home. No one, no matter how needy, was to remain hungry on the Sabbath. This, too, contributed to the feeling of equality prevailing between poor and rich. Everybody is royalty on the Sabbath. To spare nothing where the Sabbath is concerned tells more than a hundred witnesses about the scale of values that governed the Jewish way of life.

> All one's food is allocated to him [from heaven] from the beginning of the year. Not included in the budget however, is the expenditure incurred for the Sabbath and festivals and the money spent in tuition for one's children. If one goes over the allotted budget in those – he will surely be repaid from heaven.[83]

The place of money in relation to the Sabbath on the scale of values is proven even more by the tremendous financial sacrifices Jews readily made for the sake of the Sabbath. In most parts of Europe and America, it is Saturday, the day before the Christian Sunday, that is the main day for shopping and trading. Yet – no matter at what financial loss – come Sabbath, all business immediately stops. No buying, no selling – Sabbath is here and no money in the world can equal her value.

Indeed, this practice is much older than the Jewish sojourn in Christian Europe. A similar picture is drawn by Nehemiah in the fifth century B.C.E.

> In those days I saw in Judah some treading wine presses on the Sabbath and bringing in heaps of corn, etc. And it came to pass that when the gates of Jerusalem began to be dark before the Sabbath, I commanded that the doors should be shut and commanded that they should not be opened till after the Sabbath.[84]

It is surely not accidental that one of the earliest commandments on the Sabbath states: "Six days shall you work and on the seventh rest. In plowing and harvest shall you rest."[85] It comes to emphasize specifically that no "seasonal" pressure of plowing or harvest can take the Sabbath away from you. Even in the height of the agricultural, commercial, or industrial season, Sabbath comes first.

Two Versions

The Ten Commandments, which are almost universally accepted as a basic ethical code of conduct to this day, appear twice in the Pentateuch, in the second book, Exodus, and in the fifth book, Deuteronomy.

The two versions are, as expected, almost identical, as they are both framed in the same story describing the event which took place at Sinai. I said "almost" identical because there is one obvious exception and that is in regard to the fourth commandment, the one relating to the Sabbath. Here we find quite a number of important differences between the two versions, as we can see when we put the two versions of this commandment next to each other.

The first change is in the very first word of the commandment. While in Exodus it reads *zachor* – "remember," in Deuteronomy it reads *shamor* – "observe," or keep. The other major change is that in the Exodus version the reason for the observance

Version A:
Exodus 20: 8–11

Remember the Sabbath day to keep it holy. Six days shalt thou labor, and do all thy work; but the seventh day is a Sabbath unto the Lord thy God; in it thou shalt not do any manner of work, thou, nor thy son, nor thy daughter, nor thy man-servant, nor thy maid-servant, nor thy cattle, nor the stranger that is within thy gates; for in six days the Lord made heaven and earth, the sea, and all that in them is, and rested on the seventh day; wherefore the Lord blessed the Sabbath, and hallowed it.

Version B:
Deut. 5: 12–15

Observe the Sabbath day, to keep it holy, as the Lord thy God commanded thee. Six days shalt thou labor, and do all thy work; but on the seventh day is a Sabbath unto the Lord thy God; in it thou shalt not do any manner of work, thou, nor thy son, nor thy daughter, nor thy man-servant, nor thy maid-servant, nor thine ox, nor thine ass, nor any of thy cattle, nor the stranger that is within thy gates; that thy man-servant and thy maid-servant may rest as well as thou. And thou shalt remember thou wast a servant in the land of Egypt, and the Lord thy God brought thee out thence by a mighty hand and by an outstretched arm; therefore the Lord thy God commanded thee to keep the Sabbath day.

of the Sabbath is theocentric and universal: remember the Sabbath for in six days the Lord made heaven and earth, etc. In the Deuteronomy version it is anthropocentric and particularistic: keep the Sabbath in order that your man-servant and maid-servant shall rest as you do, because of your own experience of having been a slave. The fact that God rested on the Sabbath in creating the universe is not mentioned here. Myth and mystery of early beginnings give way to memory of more recent historical events.

The variations in the text were not overlooked, of course, in Jewish tradition.[86] Nor were they ever taken as representing two different "sources" or "documents." The verse "God has spoken once – twice have I heard this,"[87] has been applied to this case with the conclusion that *Zachor v'shamor b'dibur echad ne'emru, "Zachor* and *shamor* were uttered as one word."[88] Accordingly, it is not at all impossible for God to pronounce both "remember" and "keep" in one utterance – something which ordinary mortals can not do, nor grasp. Doing this He wanted to impress on us two aspects of the Sabbath, which taken simultaneously represent the full impact of the day.

Likewise, the two "reasons" for the Sabbath, the one from creation and the one from liberation, are not mutually exclusive. Both are present together to be remembered – or rather to be re-experienced – on each and every Sabbath. Creation culminating with Sabbath and liberation represent both divine and human freedom. This is clearly stated in the opening statement of the Sabbath liturgy, the *kiddush* (see further in "Perfection and Partnership") which ushers in the day with its twofold characteristics, recited over a cup of wine:

> ...Thou has graciously given us Thy holy Sabbath as a heritage *in remembrance of the creation...* the first among the holy convocations *to recall the exodus from Egypt.*

Both creation and liberation from bondage are to be re-experienced and celebrated on the Sabbath. The two versions of the Decalogue (the "Ten Words," also known as the "Ten Commandments") do not contradict, but rather supplement each other.

"*Observe* the Sabbath to keep it holy" is *not* the same as "*Remember* the Sabbath to keep it holy." What both have in common is the one purpose – to keep it, or to make it, holy. How does one make a day holy? The answer is in both "observe" and "remember." In action as well as in thought. It seems that one by itself will not suffice to achieve this purpose. Commentators over many generations have endeavored to delve into the deeper meaning of these two words and the difference between them. *Zachor* – "remember" – say some of the early Rabbis, is a "positive" commandment, while *shamor* – "keep" – is a negative one, concerned mainly with the "thou shalt not" of the Sabbath. It is in this latter sense that slavery in Egypt is emphasized and the interesting interpretation is offered "that thy man-servant and thy maid-servant may rest *kamo-kha – as well as you.*"[89] *Kamo-kha* may also mean because they *are* as well as you. *Kamo-kha*, the Hebrew word used here, is also found in the well-known commandment in Leviticus: "Love thy fellow human being *kamo-kha* (as yourself)."[90] There, too, the right meaning is not necessarily that you should like him as you like yourself, but because he is *kamo-kha*, he is like yourself a human being, with personal dignity and sensitivity, just as you yourself are. So are your man-servant and your maid-servant *kamo-kha*, human beings just like yourself.

Keep and Remember— Honor and Delight

Thus "keep" and "remember" refer to two distinct concepts, which fused together became the cornerstone for a full understanding of the Sabbath as well as of many other practices of Judaism. While "keep" stands for the Law, without which there is no Sabbath notwithstanding noble sentiments, "remember" stands for love.

While "keep" is the body of the Sabbath, "remember" is its soul – yearning and longing for the Sabbath. "Keep" is represented in the symbolic imagery of the Sabbath as a "Queen." "Remember" is represented in the same imagery as the "Bride." Both Queen and Bride are frequently used as appellations for the Sabbath in the liturgy, rabbinic literature, and poetry. Human beings respect and honor a queen; we long for and delight in the loving presence of a bride. On the Sabbath our sentiments merge to experience both dignity and delight. Every custom practiced on the Sabbath expresses this synthesis. The first one to put it into words was none other than the prophet Isaiah:

> If thou restrain thy foot because of the Sabbath from pursuing thy business on My holy day, and call the Sabbath a delight, the holy day of the Lord honorable, and shall honor it by not doing nor pursuing thy own ways nor speaking of vain matters, then shalt thou delight thyself in the Lord and I will cause you to rise upon the high places of the earth.[91]

"To honor the Sabbath" became the fountainhead of many Sabbath laws and customs, as did "to delight in the Sabbath." To mention just a few of them: we "honor" the Sabbath by bathing, taking a haircut or a shave and changing garments before the beginning of the Sabbath; we "delight" in her, eating three festive meals, singing Sabbath songs, relaxing in sleep in a way we cannot do during the week. In a paradoxical way these bodily delights and seemingly external honors bring us into the inner sanctum of the holiness of Sabbath. It is one of the many paradoxes by which the Jewish people live. It is a paradox that works and plays a major role in what helps make the Sabbath a different day, a special day – in other words, a day ready to be a vehicle for the sacred, a day of holiness – *Shabbat Kodesh.*

To "remember" one day out of all days sounds an easy assignment, but it is not as simple as it may sound. Nothing whatsoever changes in the ongoing, routine course of nature during the seventh day of the week. Heaven and earth are the same as they were all week. The act of sanctification, or setting aside, of that day takes place solely within – inspired by a secret, shared revelation between God and the individual. Nothing external serves to remind us of the day and we could overlook it, just as we might conceivably overlook a birthday or an anniversary, which we wholeheartedly meant to observe.

"Remember the Sabbath!" This despite the pressures of work, business, or play which engulf us and make it all too simple to forget that another week of life has passed and that it is time to pause before a new beginning.

Remembering the Sabbath is more complicated than it sounds. Sometimes it is a valiant feat bordering on the impossible. It is, nonetheless, possible, when a strong will and an unshakable faith are present.

Take for instance the story of Yosef Mendelowitz, imprisoned for ten years in a Soviet jail for the "crime" of attempting to escape to Israel. All the years in prison he held out and succeeded not only in not working on the Sabbath day, but – under unbelievably adverse conditions – he even managed to celebrate the day and call it holy.

Here is a description of how Yosef Mendelowitz and his friends "remembered" the Sabbath, taken from his book *Operation – Wedding*, which tells the heroic story of Jewish life in a Soviet prison.

While the other fifty prisoners in the long barrack chattered noisily, shouted, and played card games, Yosef and three of his friends went to a corner wearing their Sabbath best. His own special Sabbath garment consisted of a white undershirt his father had sent him and which he pulled over his prisoner's uniform every Sabbath during the ten years of his internment.

He and his friends said the prayers from memory and then took out the special delicacies they had sequestered during the week: omelets made from Israeli-produced egg powder; an onion fried in soya oil, also from Israel; soup made from a bouillon cube; and even herring – a real feast!

Together, Yosef and his friends recited the *kiddush* and made the blessing for the "fruit of the vine" over a handful of raisins and made the blessing over the bread. The rest of the ritual celebration consisted of some quietly-hummed songs and lots of conversation about one subject: Israel.

The other inmates were bursting with envy and someone rose to inform on them – prisoners were not allowed to form groups of more than three.

Some of the inmates, tells Yosef, had long since deteriorated into lower creatures and were unable to understand how the Jews preserved their identity under such conditions. They devoured their lard and butter like gluttons and guzzled down vodka. Yet, in comparison, even to them, the Jewish table seemed inestimably richer.

> Our modest fare was envied because we sat down to eat our meal together with the entire Jew-

> ish people who kept the Sabbath day holy.
>
> It puzzled them and they plied us with questions. "Why do you cease all work on the Sabbath? Why don't you eat pork? Why do you want to go to Israel?"
>
> "Thus were we commanded" – we answered.

To Yosef Mendelowitz and his friends in the Soviet jail, the dual command "Remember the Sabbath day to make it holy" and "Keep the Sabbath day to make it holy" was an almost superhuman challenge. They staked their lives on it and were sustained by it. Both the "remembering" and the "keeping," under the circumstances in which they found themselves, brought out the inner light and the unfathomed heroism which was in them. It helped them reach the stage when they could tell about it, as free Jews living in the hills of Jerusalem.

To say there is no genuine sadness in the world would be a lie, to close our eyes to tragedy would breed callousness and cruelty. The Sabbath does not "do away" with sadness and sorrow, it merely requires that all sadness be "tabled" for one day so that we may not forget that there is also joy and happiness in the world and acquire a more balanced and hopeful picture of life.

Two of the sons of Rav Meir (2nd century C.E.) died, or were killed, as the Sabbath was coming in. Bruriah, the wife of Rav Meir, covered them and did not tell their father of the tragedy until the Sabbath was over.[92] All laws of mourning are suspended during the Sabbath. The mourner, confined to his solitary grief during the first days of mourning, rejoins the community on the Sabbath.

In a custom practiced in Jerusalem, two lay leaders of the congregation go out towards the mourner as he interrupts his *shiva* mourning to go to the synagogue to receive the Sabbath. They meet him and escort him into the synagogue. It takes tremendous psychological stamina, but we have seen numerous cases where it was made to work, and what a therapeutic effect it had on the desperate bereaved person.

Abraham Heschel calls the Sabbath an "island." In the tempestuous ocean of time and toil there are islands of stillness where we may enter a harbor and reclaim our dignity. The island is the seventh day, the Sabbath, a day of detachment from things, instruments, and practical affairs; a day of attachment to the spirit.

On the Sabbath we do not pray explicitly for a sick friend or relative to recover, or mention cases liable to bring on depression or distress.[93] The Sabbath, by its very being, comforts and heals.

Rest Is a Created Thing

Refraining from labor is only one aspect of the Sabbath. To rest on it is another, and the two are not one and the same.

If, in resting on the Sabbath, we are to emulate the kind of rest God took after the six days of creation, we must find out what "rest" means in relation to God. He certainly does not get fatigued or require rest in order to go on working. Nor is it feasible that God ordains us to rest only out of concern that we should not get overtired. According to Rabbinic legend,[94] Moses tried to "sell" the idea of the Sabbath to Pharaoh, prior to the exodus, convincing him that the slaves would do a better job if granted a day off. Indeed, this was an argument to tempt a slave-driver like Pharaoh, but it is not mentioned at all when ordaining the Sabbath to the Israelites, or anywhere else in the Bible. The rest that we are required to attain on the Sabbath is an aim in itself, a God-like rest referred to in the liturgy (Sabbath afternoon service) as *Menuhah*

Shleima, "a perfect rest, that You God require...a rest that comes from You."

A rest that comes from the Almighty is not a rest that comes automatically by cessation from work. It is created and given to us by God Himself for us to create again by observing the Sabbath.

The words: "On the seventh day God finished His work,"[95] seem to present a problem. Does it not also say: "He rested on the seventh day" and "in six days the Lord made heaven and earth,"[96] which should make it clear that on the sixth day God finished His work. Why "on the seventh" in the earlier reference?

The Rabbis of the Midrash solved this by suggesting that the sixth is not the final day of creation and that there actually was an act of creation on the seventh day. Just as heaven and earth were created in six days, *menuhah* was created on the seventh and is to be created again every Sabbath.

> After six days of creation what did the universe lack? *Menuhah.* Came the Sabbath, came *menuhah* and the universe was complete. And what is this *menuhah* that God created on the seventh day? Tranquility, ease, peace, and quiet.[97]

Menuhah, says Rabbi Abraham Joshua Heschel, the concept which we usually render with "rest," means much more than freedom from toil, strain, or activity of any kind. *Menuhah* is not a negative concept but something real and intrinsically positive. It took a special act of creation to bring it into being, for the universe would be incomplete without it. To the biblical mind, *menuhah* is the same as happiness and stillness, with no fear and no distrust.

In one of the psalms recited on the Sabbath, we read:

The Lord is my shepherd.
I shall not want.
He maketh me to lie down
in green pastures:
He leadeth me beside the waters of *menuhot.*[98]

It is on the Sabbath, the day of *menuhah* that we may come near the green pastures, beside the waters of *menuhot*, soothing, calming, inspiring.

Erich Fromm, the famed psychologist-philosopher, in analyzing the symbolism of the Sabbath noticed rightly that "the idea that man should rest from his work one day every week sounds like a self-evident, social-hygienic measure to give man the physical and spiritual rest and relaxation he needs in order not to be swallowed up by his daily work."[99] This explanation, says Fromm, is true as far as it goes, but it does not answer some questions which arise if we pay close attention to the Sabbath law of the Bible and particularly to the Sabbath ritual as it developed in the post-biblical tradition. What then is the answer arising out of the symbolism inherent in the restricting rituals of the Sabbath laws?

The essential point Fromm makes is that the concept of work underlying the biblical and the later talmudic concept is not simply that of physical effort but can be defined thus: "Work" is any interference by humanity, be it constructive or destructive, with the physical world. "Rest" is a state of peace between humanity and nature. Human beings must leave nature untouched, not changed in any way, neither by building nor by destroying anything. Even the smallest change made by man in the natural process is a violation of "rest." The Sabbath is the day of peace between humanity and nature; work is a kind of disturbance of the humanity-nature equilibrium. On the basis of this general definition, we can understand the Sabbath ritual. Indeed, any heavy work such as plowing or building is work in this, as well as in our modern, sense. But lighting a match and pulling up a grass blade, while not requiring effort, are symbols of human interference with the natural process, are a breach of peace between humanity and nature.

On the basis of this principle, says Fromm, we understand also the talmudic prohibition against carrying something of even light weight on our person. In fact, the carrying of anything as such is not forbidden. I can carry a heavy load within my house or my estate without violating the Sabbath ritual. But I must not carry even a handkerchief from one domain to another, for instance from the private domain of the house to the public domain of the street.[100] This law is an extension of the idea of peace from the natural to the social realm. Just as we must not interfere with or change the natural equilibrium, we must refrain from changing the social order. That means not only cessation from business, but also the avoidance of the most primitive form of transference of property, namely its local transference from one domain to another.

The Sabbath symbolizes, according to Fromm, a state of complete harmony between humanity and nature and between one person and another. By not working, that is to say, by not participating in the process of natural and social change, we are free from the chains of nature and from the chains of time, even if only for one day a week.

Resting, asserts Fromm, has a meaning different from the modern meaning of relaxation. In the state of rest, human beings anticipate the state of human freedom. On the Sabbath the relationship of humanity with nature and of one person with another is one of harmony, of peace, of noninterference. Work is a symbol of conflict, competition, and disharmony; rest is an expression of dignity, peace, and freedom.

The Sabbath ritual occupies such a central place in the biblical religion because it is more than a "day of rest" in the modern sense; it is a symbol of salvation and freedom. This also explains God's rest; this rest is not necessary because God is tired, but expresses the idea that great as the world's creation is, the greater and crowning creation is peace. God's work is a condescension; God must "rest" not out of exhaustion, but because He is free and fully God only when He has created His work. So we are fully ourselves only when we do not work, when we are at peace with nature and humanity. That is why the Sabbath commandment is at one time motivated by God's rest and at the other by the liberation from Egypt. Both mean the same and interpret each other; rest *is* freedom.

This analysis by Erich Fromm of the symbolism of the Sabbath was contested by Rabbi Walter Wurzburger. In his view, the concept of *melakhah*, the work forbidden on the Sabbath and its strict limitation of what falls under the scope of "work," seems to rule out such a humanistic, idyllic reading of the Sabbath.

The *halakhic* definition of *melakhah*, not as mere labor, but as purposeful work points, according to Wurzburger, to the specific religious dimension of the Sabbath, which transcends the realm of social and psychological utility. If prophets such as Isaiah and later on the Rabbis could look upon the observance of the Sabbath as the central axis of all of Judaism, it was because they saw in it the crystallization of the most basic Jewish tenets regarding our relationship to nature and God. Viewed from this vantage point, the prohibition against "purposeful activity" emerges as a much-needed reminder to us that we, too, are merely creatures of God. We must beware lest we become intoxicated with our success in conquering nature and fall victim to arrogant self-idolization. To be sure, human creativity and mastery over nature represent perfectly legitimate activities. We Jews have never shared the stance of the Promethean myth which condemns human creativity as an act of defiance against heavenly powers. But with all our endorsement of human creativity which has produced the miracles of civilization, we recognize the debilitating spiritual hazards that loom in the wake of our triumphs over nature. We are apt to forget that the universe – including our own capacity for creativity – is not a self-contained unit, but belongs to the Creator. Because of the regularity and order prevailing within the realm of nature, we are prone – especially in the "secular city" – to overlook the divine source of all existence. Thus, the Sabbath saves us from the idolatry of science and technology. It reveals what nature conceals: the world is not a self-sufficient cosmos, but the continuous creation of God.

This theme is stressed in Exodus where it is affirmed that "the seventh day is the Sabbath unto God and thou shalt not perform any kind of work."[101] No mention is made here of rest, relaxation, or other human benefits. The emphasis here is unmistakably theocentric. Humanity, as it were, is put in its place. The Sabbath makes us realize that we have a legitimate right to harness the forces of nature for creative work only if we refrain from self-deification and look upon ourselves as creatures charged by our Creator with the task of imitating Him by completing the task of creation.

This insight into the true meaning of Sabbath rest and its purpose is succinctly described by Rabbi Samuel H. Dresner: "Is man creature or creator?"[102] he asks. In our victory over the forces of nature, whose deepest secrets we unravel – turning great forests into farms and cities, drawing forth from the earth gold, silver, and precious stones, harnessing powerful rivers to provide untold energy, learning to fly through the air like a bird and swim through the water like a fish, conquering dreaded diseases that were the scourge of society for centuries, building towers that pierce the clouds and trains to carry thousands underground, splitting the atom into incomprehensible power and discovering how to ascend even to the moon – it is to be expected that we would be tempted to consider ourselves lords of all, masters of the universe. It is so easy for us to think of ourselves not as creature, but as creator – all-knowing, all-seeing, all-dominating lords of nature. Infatuated with our marvelous talents, we may forget the real Creator, without whom all our achievements are as nothing, all our gadgets dust, all our inventions instruments that can be turned into terrible weapons which can destroy, rather than improve, the world.

For the real purpose of life is not to conquer nature, but to conquer the self; not to fashion a city out of a forest, but to fashion a soul out of a human being; not to build bridges, but to build human kindness; not to learn to fly like a bird or swim like a fish, but to walk on the earth like a human being; not to erect skyscrapers, but to establish mercy and justice; not to manufacture an ingenious technical civilization, but to be holy in the midst of unholiness. The real tasks are to learn how to remain civilized in the midst of insanity, how to retain a share of our dignity in the midst of the Dachaus and Buchenwalds, how to keep the mark of Cain from obscuring the image of the divine, how to fashion a home of love and peace, how to create children obedient and reverent, how to find the strength to perform the *mitzvot*, how to bend our will to God's will.

It is the Sabbath that comes to remind us of all this. Six days a week we compete with the natural world – building, subduing, struggling to overcome. On the Sabbath we declare *menuhah*, take temporary leave from the stressful world, while remaining very much attached to it; declare *menuhah*, accept gladly the rest that was given to us, rest created by God for himself and for us. This rest does not come when we decide that we are in a state of exhaustion, or when our duties at work permit us to "take off" a few days. It comes completely independent of us, with the sunset of Friday afternoon, as it did in the very beginning and as it will continually, "a sign forever."

Sabbath and the Modern Problem of Leisure

The significance of *menuhah* (rest) is emphasized throughout the Sabbath liturgy. Three times we pray, "Our God and God of our fathers, be pleased with our *menuhah.*" We ask God to accept it and to be pleased with it, as though our *menuhah* were a form of divine worship, as are sacrifices. Obviously, we are not dealing with a mere self-indulgent vacation, invoking God's maternal approval of our concern with our health. The *minhah* prayer, which celebrates the qualities of *menuhah*, concludes its central portion on this note: "...and by means of (Israel's) *menuhah*, they sanctify Thy Name." Sabbath rest is thus nothing less than a vehicle for the observance of Judaism's most illustrious precept, *kiddush ha-Shem*, "the sanctification of the divine Name." To "sanctify the Name" means to act in such a manner that glory will redound to Judaism and enhance the Name (i.e., reputation) of the God of Israel in the world. Obviously, we are dealing with something far more fundamental than merely taking a day off from work every week. There lies within *menuhah* a concept that Jews were meant to teach to all humankind (unlike the *halakhic* observance of the prohibition of *melakhah* which was covenanted just for Israel), the appreciation of which will add to the glory of God and Torah. We are dealing, in other words, with a Jewish ideal of universal import and relevance. As such, its implications must extend beyond those of mere relaxation.

According to Rabbi Norman Lamm, on whose thorough essay on the subject this chapter is based, authentic *menuhah* requires that on the Sabbath we direct our creative abilities not toward nature but toward ourselves, spiritually and intellectually. *Menuhah* is not a suspension for one day of the week of our creative energies, but a refocusing of our creative talents upon ourselves. The difference between the prohibited *melakhah* and the recommended *menuhah* lies not in the *fact* of creativity, but in the *object* of one's creative powers: whether directed toward oneself or one's environment, the inner world or the outer world.

The same idea in slightly different phrasing can give us, says Rabbi Lamm, a new insight into an enormously important contemporary problem. *Menuhah* is, in a sense, religiously enforced leisure. It is the available time we take away from our normal labor. If we now rephrase our question about the nature of *menuhah*, the problem is whether leisure is to be considered negatively – time taken off from work – or positively; and if positively, how? Is this leisure-*menuhah* a vacuum of inactivity, or can it and should it become a higher form of activity?

The problem of leisure is of crucial importance for our society. Irwin Edman, the late professor of aesthetics at Columbia, once said that the best test of a civilization is the quality of its leisure. If you want to know what a civilization is really like, look not only at its technological and artistic production, but see how its members spend their weekends. That will provide a more reliable criterion of the nature of a people. Professor Edman was anticipated in this by the Talmud, which tells us that a person's character can be tested in three ways: *be'kiso, be'koso, u've'kaaso.* "By his pocket" – is the person a miser or a spendthrift: "by his cup" – how does the person respond to the temptation of alcoholic excesses; "and by his temper" – can the person exercise self-control in the presence of provocation? These three provide a guide to what kind of character a person possesses. But there is a fourth test according to some, a fourth index of character or personality: *be'sahako*, "by his play" – how does he use his leisure? That will reveal a person's essential quality.

The use of leisure is more than a criterion of our social health. It is an urgent problem that must be solved in order to avoid major crises that threaten the whole structure of our society. Increasing automation, and also early retirement combined with growing longevity, are bound to make more and more time available to most of us. Now, what is going to happen with the new surplus of leisure as more and more man-hours are released from office and factory? The Southern California Research Council recently predicted that soon the typical worker in the U.S.A. will have the choice of a twenty-five-week vacation, retirement at age thirty-eight, or a twenty-two-hour work week. If this indeed becomes a reality in the next few years, as it shows every promise of doing, what in heaven's name will people do with all that spare time? Cultivate the soul and mind, or dull their brains and fill their cranial cavities with that ceaseless flow of tripe and terror that issues from television and other channels of mass communication? Or worse yet, will they seek the cheap thrills of social, moral and legal delinquency?

When the Torah describes God as "resting" (which should never be taken anthropomorphically), it says *shavat va'yinafah. Shavat*, "He rested," is similar to the Shabbat, and it means to refrain from work. *Shevitah* (the noun which in contemporary Hebrew also means "a strike") is a period in which we desist from work. The negative, passive aspect is immediately evident. The second word is *va'yinafash* (noun: *nofesh*). This signifies another form of leisure. *Ve-yinafash* or *nofesh* comes from the word *nefesh*: the soul, the spirit.

Hence, the concept of *menuhah* contains one

or both of these ideas. The negative understanding of *menuhah* (or leisure) we may call *shevitah*, cessation of activity. The positive we may call *nofesh*. (*Shevitah* is not used in a pejorative sense, because both of these signify proper uses of leisure).

Shevitah means we cease our usual labors and this respite from routine work activity allows us to rediscover ourselves by emerging from the work week. Over-involved in and overwhelmed by our set pattern of work, our dignity is threatened. We begin to identify ourselves by the functions we perform in society or family, and turn into impersonal ciphers, like beasts of burden that can be easily replaced by any function-bearing animal that happens to be technologically efficient. By disengaging from our involvement with nature, with society, with business, we are permitted self-expression. Our real "self" comes to the fore. We do not have to be busy taking notes, or selling, or buying, or fighting. By means of *shevitah* on our Sabbath day of "rest," we can start expressing the real self that lies within. *Shevitah* is thus the use of leisure to restore our individuality in all its integrity. By pulling out of the routine of weekday involvement, we confront ourselves in order to find out who we are. Leisure helps us resolve our "identity crises."

By eschewing normal activities, which harness us during the week into Pavlovian conditioned responses – completely deterministic behaviors – the inner, original ego emerges. We can rediscover ourselves when we are removed from the matrix of these challenges and their expected responses. In this sense, *shevitah* exploits the limits of our character and potential. (As we shall see shortly, it *exploits* them, but it cannot *expand* them.)

In practical terms, leisure is a time for games. Leisure refers not only to *time*, but also to the *nature* of the activity. You can drive a car and it can be part of your work, if you are a taxi driver; but you can also drive and consider it leisure. If you are a professor or student, you may look upon study as work, but you can also look upon study as a delight and a joy – whether you are a taxi driver in the one case or an intellectual in the other. Leisure is gaming in the highest sense. It places a person in a new environment, in new conditions, and allows that person to bring out unsuspected skills heretofore latent, to find new ways of expression – in aesthetics or athletics or any other activity which is unaccustomed during the week.

From here we take the next step, *nofesh*. *Nofesh* is more than self-discovery; it is the use of leisure for self-transformation. Paradoxically, it is in a sense more passive than *shevitah*. Instead of activity for the purpose of self-expression, it may require a certain kind of personal, inner silence in which we makes ourselves available for a higher impression. It is the incorporation of the transcendent, rather than the articulation of the immanent. You try to respond to something that comes from without, from above. *Nofesh* does not mean to fulfill yourself but to go outside yourself, to rise beyond yourself; not to discover your identity, but rather to create a new and better identity. Very often we find people, especially young people, who complain "I don't know who I am." The answer to those people is: "You probably aren't! Your job is to *create* an 'I' to do something in order to *make* a self." You're not going to find out who you are by moping "Who am I?" and by scrutinizing your face as you look into the mirror. Your task is not to discover, but to invent an 'I'. That's the real problem. That is what *nofesh* is all about. *Nofesh* requires of us that we take our creative talents, which during the week are applied to impersonal nature or unengaged society, and turn them inwards to create a new, real self. This is the inner and deeper meaning of *menuhah.* It is re-creation, not relaxation.

Our tradition speaks of a very interesting phenomenon concerning the Sabbath. During the week everyone has a *neshamah*, a soul. But on the Sabbath we receive a *neshamah yeterah*, an "additional soul." This suggests that there is some kind of undeveloped facet of personality, a spiritual dimension, of which we remain unaware in the normal course of events. On Shabbat (in the *nofesh* sense of a *menuhah*) we are given the time to enrich ourselves by developing or creating this extra spiritual dimension.

Hence, whereas *shevitah* implies the development of a latent, pre-existent talent, *nofesh* means the creation of a novelty within the personality, bringing something new in, transforming the self by growing into a *neshamah yeterah.*

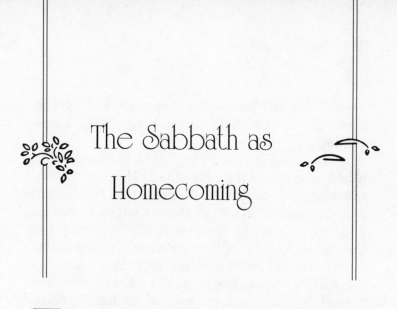

The Sabbath as Homecoming

The root of the Hebrew word from which Sabbath derives closely resembles another root in Hebrew carrying the connotation of "returning" or "coming home."

This linguistic fact, as well as a certain unusual way of spelling one of the words in the biblical passage concerning the Sabbath[103] contributed to the association of the Sabbath in the Hebrew mind with the idea of returning, of coming home. This idea found many expressions in the course of Jewish thinking, one especially influenced by Kabbalah and Hassidism.

Jewish mysticism saw our world as broken and shattered and on its way to be "mended" (*tikun*) by the combined aspiration and directed action of God and humanity. While our present state of being is fractured and splintered, often fragmented to the degree of incoherence, wholeness and perfection are our destination. Our present state of being denotes "exile" (*galut*), temporary displacement; its end, however, marks "redemption" (*geulah*), homecoming.

Threefold is the "exile" which plagues this world: first comes the exile of God Himself, the displacement of the Divine Presence (the *Shekhinah*) from its proper place. In the metaphor of Jewish mysticism, it is the separation which occurred in the divine cosmic sphere between the masculine aspect and the feminine aspect of the Godhead – the painful estrangement of the "King" from the "Queen." This exile is pictured as having taken place in cosmic space.

The second "exile" transpired in historic time, and refers to the exile of the people of Israel from its land. This has been viewed as a temporary situation to be terminated "any day" with the return of the people to their true home.

The third "exile," which came to its fullest expression in the thought and literature of modernity, but which was amply described much earlier in Jewish thought, is the exile of the person. The alienated individual, estranged from his immediate environment, unsure of himself, feels lost and caught up in a hostile and meaningless existence.

The Sabbath stands out as the triumphant great homecoming for all three forms of exile.

On this day, God the King meets his Bride and Queen – the Sabbath. This meeting has been glorified in Jewish mystical literature in the most sublime poetic expressions of eroticism, love and beauty. Many a symbol of the Sabbath ritual comes to reflect this divine re-unification.

For the people of Israel – wherever they were – the Sabbath was a reminder of home. All subterranean fountains of love and longing for Zion and Jerusalem came to be openly expressed during the Sabbath. It was, so to speak, an "extra-territorial" piece of the firm ground of Eretz Israel in the midst of exile in the Diaspora and dispersion.

It is interesting that the Psalm which is customarily recited prior to the grace after meals on the Sabbath is different from the one recited during the week. During the week we recite Psalm 137: "By the rivers of Babylon there we sat down and wept when we remembered Zion....How can we sing the song of the Lord in a strange land?" On the Sabbath we recite instead Psalm 126: "When the Lord returned us to Zion we were like dreamers.... Our mouths were filled with laughter and our tongues flowed with song."

Experiencing holiness in time immeasurably intensified the yearning to experience holiness in space. The Sabbath undoubtedly had much to do with awakening the Jews for the return to their land in modern times as part of the efforts of the Zionist movement. The abnormality of life in an alien environment, as a minority, even under the best conditions, came to the fore especially on the Sabbath, which set the Jew apart from the majority of the population who marked their day of rest on Friday or Sunday. On the Sabbath Jews became aware that after all they were "outsiders" and that some day they would go home.

Rabbi Mordechai Ha-Cohen tells the following story. Whether apocryphal or authentic, it is very touching and illustrates this point in the manner of a modern Midrash. It is a story about Theodor Herzl, the visionary founder of the modern Jewish state. One day, as he was walking the streets of Vienna, Herzl had an encounter which brought the first thoughts about the necessity and feasibility of a reborn Jewish State flashing into his mind. On his way he noticed an elderly person, dressed in the typical habit of an East European Hassidic Jew, standing in a corner, weeping bitterly. When Herzl inquired why he was crying, the stranger answered, "And how can I not cry – if my only son is at work today in a factory!" "What is wrong with that?" asked the astonished Herzl, who was until that time an assimilated Jew. "It is Sabbath today," came the weeping Jew's reply. "It was always my life's dream that my son find a productive and useful way of making a living. When he finally got this wonderful job in the factory, he was told that he would have to give it up if he insists on not working on the Sabbath, rather than on the official day off, which is Sunday. What should I do? How am I to decide now between my son's future and my people's Sabbath?"

At this point a tear came to Herzl's eyes. He rushed home and sat down to write *Der Judenstaat* – the classic book which established political Zionism. If Jews could have their own state, Herzl must have realized, they could be spared such painful decision-making.

Observing the Sabbath with all its restrictions is not without problems for a people energetically engaged in building, defending, and running a modern state. Nevertheless the Sabbath did indeed "come home" in the reborn State of Israel. It was declared in one of the earliest constitutional laws of the State to be the official day of rest for the State and all its operations (with a provision made for Moslem and Christian citizens of Israel to observe their own religious days of rest).

The Sabbath is rightly at home in reborn Israel. The Sabbath meant home even while Jews were (or still are) "en route," and away from home. Chaim Nahman Bialik, the great Hebrew poet, tells a beautiful story of how his family when cruelly deported from its home in a village in Tsarist Russia, found itself desolately and aimlessly wandering in a forest. Suddenly, his mother realized that it was Friday afternoon and as sunset was approaching, she immediately pulled out from somewhere two little candles, lit them, covered her face to recite the blessing over the Sabbath and all at once "we were back home again." Between the stars flickering above and the Sabbath candles flickering below, they no longer felt uprooted and ashamed. While probably realizing subconsciously that the Sabbath was bound inevitably to come to an end, they were, for the time being, in a peaceful, serene home.

In the personal sphere too, it is the Sabbath that can give the alienated individual a sense of homecoming. It was not so long ago, when Jewish artisans and peddlers, teachers and scribes, who during the week were working hard to eke out a living "on the road," would make every possible effort to be home "for *shabbes*." Yet coming home for the Sabbath always meant much more than physically returning home from work or business. It meant an "at-homeness" which would rarely be sensed during the week. The weekly Sabbath celebration brought on a family togetherness sparked with tenderness and intimacy impossible to achieve under the pressures of the weekly schedule. It gave parents the time and the relaxation to listen to their children, to talk to them, to smile at them; and it gave them time for one another.

Friday night, not unwittingly called in Hebrew *leil shabbat* ("Sabbath night") was never taken as a "free night" to "go out," as one can sleep late on the morning after. No. It was, and is, for Sabbath observers, a "night in." Very rarely does one leave home on Friday night, no matter what the occasion or whatever "function" is taking place outside. This custom must go back to Tannaitic times. The ancient Rabbis interpret the verse "And I shall give the rain of your land in its proper time"[104] – when is the "proper time" for rain? On Friday night. Do you know why? Because everyone stays home on that night and rain is not going to trouble anyone.

As the Sabbath comes, we come home from

our alienated existence in this strange world. We again encounter and honor the image of God in ourselves and in all human beings around us.

Language of Love

A series of hymns is added to the Sabbath morning liturgy in the prayerbook, and the first of them is Psalm 19 which reads:

1. *For the Leader, A Psalm of David.*
2. *The heavens declare the glory of God.*
   And the firmament shows His handiwork;
3. *Day unto day expresses His greatness;*
   Night unto night makes Him known.
4. *There is no speech, there are no words.*
   Their voice is not heard.
5. *Yet their sway extends over all the earth,*
   And their message to the ends of the world.
   In the heavens, he hath set a tent for the sun.
6. *For the sun is a bridegroom coming out of his chamber,*
   It rejoices as a strong man to run its course.
7. *Its going forth is from one end of the heaven,*
   And its circuit unto the other;
   Nothing is hidden from its heat.
8. *The law of the Lord is perfect, restoring the soul;*
   The testimony of the Lord is sure, making wise the simple.

9. *The precepts of the Lord are right, rejoicing the heart;*
The commandment of the Lord is clear, enlightening the eyes.
10. *The fear of the Lord is pure, enduring forever;*
The judgments of the Lord are true,
They are righteous altogether;
11. *More to be desired are they than gold,*
Yea, than much fine gold;
Sweeter also than honey and the honeycomb.
12. *Moreover by them is Thy servant warned;*
In keeping of them there is great reward.
13. *What man can discern his own errors?*
Clear me from hidden faults.
14. *Keep back Thy servant also from willful sins,*
That they may not have dominion over me;
Then shall I be blameless,
And I shall be clear from great transgression.
15. *May the words of my mouth*
And the meditation of my heart
Be acceptable before Thee,
O Lord, my Rock, and my Redeemer.

This Psalm presented a problem to Bible critics and commentators. They could not find the connection between its two parts (verses 1-7 and verses 8-15), dealing with two distinctly different subjects: nature with its beauty and grandeur in part one, Torah and the precepts of the Lord in part two. Not even a connecting clue could be found between the two parts, and some critics decided that we are dealing here with two separate psalms which happened to fall together by sheer accident.[105]

When viewed, however, from the vantage point of the Sabbath (see the closing stanzas: it indeed might have originally been a Sabbath prayer), one realizes the perfect cohesiveness of the Psalm. It is on the Sabbath day that we get a chance to raise our eyes upward, to marvel at the sight, and to sing, along with the Psalmist: "The heavens declare the glory of God; And the firmament shows His Handiwork."

It is on the Sabbath also that we can raise our minds from the mundane and sing, along with the Psalmist, the praises of God's Torah. It is on the Sabbath that we are able to commune with God both in His creation and His revelation. On this day we renew our bond with the majesty of nature.

As the Sabbath enters, it is customary to recite the verses of the Song of Songs, resplendent with the beautiful descriptions of hills and valleys, trees and flowers, rivers and wells. The mystics in sixteenth-century Safed used to leave the synagogue and go to the fields to welcome the Sabbath outdoors, in the lap of nature, in the "orchard of The Sacred Apples."[106]

According to an ancient custom, kept to this day in modern Israel, one adorns the Sabbath with colorful and fragrant flowers and myrtles.[107] On Friday afternoon the streets of towns and villages in modern Israel fill with hundreds of people carrying bouquets of flowers on their way home.

A renewed acquaintance with nature and its beauty is one part of the Sabbath. Another part is the renewed acquaintance with the perfect colors and sweet fragrance of Torah. Philosopher Hermann Cohen sees in the Sabbath the expression of God's love for humanity – a love affair which culminates in an everlasting covenant. The Sabbath is a gift of love. How does one respond to love? Flowers are more eloquent than words. Also, listening with rapt attention to the voice of your beloved, trying to absorb and understand your beloved's message with all of your being, is the most profound expression of your acceptance of such abundant love.

The Torah was characterized by the rabbis as a love letter God left before parting to go on a faraway journey. As a precious love letter we read it over and over again, each time discovering in it new meaning and savor. Thus was the Torah, the five books of Moses, divided up into fifty-four portions – one for every Sabbath of the year. Each week the portion of this particular Sabbath is read by all Jews, everywhere. Read, examined, studied, probed, consulted. No matter where in the world you find yourself, you will have no problem of orientation, as long as you know what the portion of the week is. It provides a subject to talk about with people you have just met, or a conversation piece between parents and children. You refer to the "portion of the week" in dating your correspondence. The portion of Torah which you will read on the forthcoming Sabbath is with you all week long. Every day. Just as the heavens are there all week and you see them on the Sabbath, so is the Torah.

The two parts of Psalm 19 are really one, so the Sabbath assures us. Perhaps the most striking expression of the genuine concept of Sabbath rest, says Rabbi Irving ("Yitz") Greenberg in his *Guide to Shabbat*,[108] is the tradition of celebrating Shabbat with sexual intercourse. A special Shabbat observance is to make love on Friday night. The Talmud relates that great scholars, if they would have sexual relations only once a week, would make sure that it take place on Friday night.[109] To have sexual intercourse is, in biblical language, to *know* someone. It is the act that combines mutual understanding and physical attraction: desire and relationship culminate in an act of union with another person that touches both partners in body and soul. Ideally, it is the confirmation in action of a total acceptance and affirmation of the uniqueness and spirituality of Shabbat. At the same time, the physical well-being, lack of pressure, and leisure of Shabbat is the perfect setting for attaining such a high degree of intimacy and openness to the other. In turn, the union enriches and deepens the individual's sense of well-being and value. Thus it strengthens the process of becoming more human on this day.

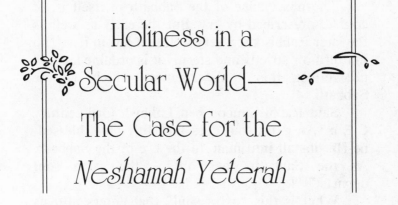

Holiness in a Secular World— The Case for the *Neshamah Yeterah*

How can you enter fully into the Sabbath? Isn't it easier said than done?

Is it truly possible to tear yourself away from the hectic pace of your life to enter into another world, a serene sanctuary in time, just because the calendar and the clock show that at this particular moment – let us say at 5:32 p.m. on Friday – the Sabbath arrives and it is time to light the candles? What is the secret strength of the soft whisper of those small flickering candles vis-a-vis the floodlights, electronic sounds, and other noises that fill our eyes and ears in their non-stop barrage? Furthermore, how can this transfer from one world to the other take place without a drastic break – without running away to a solitary resort in the mountains or to the forest – right here, in the midst of your own home, surrounded by the members of your own family and community.

The observance of the Sabbath in itself is, of course, prescribed by law. But the early as well as the later Rabbis knew very well that law in itself, no matter how strictly and sternly it is ordained, could not effect this transformation which is the Sabbath.

Said Rabbi Simeon ben Lakhish (3rd century C.E.): "An extra soul does the Holy One, blessed-be-He, install into man on the eve of the Sabbath. As the Sabbath goes out – the extra soul departs."[110]

What is this "extra soul" that enters into us together with the onset of the Sabbath? Following the metaphoric language of Rabbi Nachman in *Zohar Chadash*,[111] we may say that it is the holy spirit which is within us, and which comes to the fore on the Sabbath. It is also according to the same source the invisible crown that human beings all wear, similar to the crown worn by the ministering angels. The Sabbath comes to remind us of this holy spirit, this extra dimension of our soul, which is within us, and which we keep imprisoned for six days of toil. It comes to open our eyes to see the holy crown above us which we barred our eyes from seeing during the six days.

Just as in the beginning, when Adam was first created, he was no more than a lump of dust until the Lord breathed into him a "spirit of life" and made him into a "living soul,"[112] so we still use only part of *our* spiritual potential until the "extra soul" is breathed into us as the Sabbath enters.

The saintly Rabbi Haim of Czernowitz, scholar and mystic, lived at about the same time as the Baal Shem Tov and devoted a great part of his Torah study and writing to the Sabbath. In addition to his famous work *Beer Mayim Hayim* ("A Fountain of Living Water") he also wrote a volume entitled *Sidduro shel Shabbat* ("The Order of the Sabbath"). Eyewitnesses who knew him told that on every Sabbath, from the moment Sabbath entered until it departed, he grew a head taller than his usual weekday height.

Knowing what Sabbath meant to Reb Hayim, I am not surprised and have no difficulty believing it.

Sabbath comes to tell us that every one has the ability to rise above his or her self, to transcend to a higher level of life, of dignity and of delight. Do we dare shut ourselves up in our confined slave's cell and deny this assertion of human freedom which the Sabbath pronounces in our ears every seventh day? Can we say, in all honesty, that we never ever personally experienced some glimpse of Jacob's dream of "a ladder standing on the ground with its top reaching heaven?"

Rav Pinchas of Koritz says: "A ladder standing on the ground" – these are the six days of the week; "its top reaching heaven" – the Sabbath.

Even in this most secular, technological, pragmatic, and materialistic world, it seems to be impossible to exorcise completely our dream of an ascending ladder, which stands on earth and touches heaven. It seems impossible to confine ourselves to life imprisonment in our limited materialistic existence. When the lights of freedom all around us are dimmed, when we are about to lose touch with dignity and delight, the Sabbath comes and calls out to us: Don't forget who you are! Remember I am here! Please let me in, please! I am queen, be my king for a day. I am your bride, be my lover again.

The Sabbath is the only commandment that does not depend on human action. The festivals are contingent on the fixing of the calendar, calculated by human beings; the performance of all other *mitzvot* relies upon some human endeavor.[113] But the Sabbath, declared once by God, comes and goes at regular intervals without any human intervention; she cannot be stopped or postponed. It remains up to us, however, to let her in, to receive her properly, to acknowledge that indeed we do have an extra dimension to our being. For, if we are not more than what we are – we are, most likely, less than what we are.

Why must one necessarily accomplish this climb upward on the Sabbath? Why not choose just any day at one's convenience to make a Sabbath for oneself?

This, in itself, might certainly be a noble idea. Forgetting for a moment the religious, cosmic significance of the Sabbath, how many of us would be capable of attaining a high level of spirituality without the support of tradition and community? There are, of course, people, individuals, who can live their lives in ongoing high spiritual tension and intensity – but can we all? And for how long can we sustain such intensity alone?

Even the cosmic historical Sabbath, a built-in foundation stone of Jewish civilization and culture for thousands of years, is still struggling for its place in the routine life of society and the individual. This struggle for the life of the Sabbath was no secret to the Rabbis and teachers, fathers, mothers, and children who sought in every generation new ways and means to make the celebration of the Sabbath possible in a world governed more and more by materialism and secularism. Penetrating into the deeper meaning of the Sabbath for their life and the life of their people, appreciating more and more the preciousness of this heavenly gift, they designed ever new ideas and customs, which have become part and parcel of Jewish culture. It would surely be senseless for anyone coming from this rich culture to blindly discard this prolific depository, audaciously claiming to build a "new" culture and spiritual life "from scratch." While not everything in Jewish tradition could nor should be transplanted "lock, stock, and barrel" to our own life, the Sabbath and most of its practices are definitely transferable to the modern world. In many respects, they are even more vitally needed for us today than they were for our ancestors yesterday.

If *kadosh* – "holy" – means "special," "separate," "set aside," we cannot remain passive, apathetic as this special day comes to enwrap us and lift us up to another, higher level of existence. That has been self-evident to Jews through the generations. Although they believed beyond any doubt that the Sabbath is a divine gift to humanity, they realized and taught that humanity has to participate actively in making this gift meaningful.

They understood the verse: "And the children of Israel shall keep the Sabbath... *la'asot et ha'shabbat*"[114] to mean that one is not told only to keep the Sabbath, but also to "make it." It is indeed they who made the Sabbath what it is. They also believed and taught that the "extra soul" we receive on the Sabbath is not merely a figure of speech, but a reality. What did they mean by it? How did they conceive of it?

Seven Branches, Six Trumpets

Let us mention but a few of the ways Jews have employed in this creative process of "making" the Sabbath – ways which could be as effective for us today as they were for our ancestors.

Instead of satisfying ourselves with reminiscing nostalgically about how beautiful "was" the Sabbath that we remember from childhood, and making our own Sabbath profane, we can, if we wish, bequeath something to our children and grandchildren so that when they mature they, too, can recall with fondness *our* Sabbath. The preservation of culture and transmission of the wisdom of life consists not only in being ready and capable to learn from our grandparents, but just as much in being able to transmit it to our grandchildren.

Sabbath, our ancestors knew, does not come to us suddenly. It requires mental and practical preparation. Firstly, it must be regarded as the living center of the week and not as a sluggish week end. It is worth noting here that the days of the week have no names in the Hebrew language. They are counted as *yom rishon b'shabbat* – "the first day towards the Sabbath"; *yom sheni b'shabbat* – "the second day towards the Sabbath"; and so on, until Friday – "the sixth day towards the Sabbath" which is also called *erev shabbat*, "the eve of the Sabbath"; and then: *Shabbat.*

The Talmud tells us about some great Rabbis many centuries ago, whose custom was to buy any choice piece of food they found in the market during the weekdays and put it away to be eaten on the Sabbath.

For hundreds of years Jewish homemakers saw to it that the Sabbath meals (three meals are mandatory, based on Exodus 16:25 – "eat it today," etc., where the word "today" is repeated three times) should include the choicest dishes, some of which are offered only on Sabbath, never on a weekday. At least one of the dishes eaten on the Sabbath should be *personally* cooked or baked by *you*, the man or the woman receiving the Sabbath. Even great talmudic scholars, we are told, took a personal part in the preparation of food for the Sabbath.

The Sabbath, to be sure, is not confined to the Sabbath day itself, but permeates every day of the week. We follow all week long the weekly portion of the Torah which is then read as part of the Sabbath synagogue service. Jewish mysticism sees the days of the week as "branches" while the "roots" are in the Sabbath. It is the source from whence

God's grace comes every day. In the *Zohar*, the classic book of Kabbalah, the days of the week are pictured in the shape of a seven-branched candelabrum, a menorah, with the Sabbath as its middle shaft and the days of the week surrounding it on both sides. In our illustration, Wednesday, Thursday and Friday are on the left, and Sunday, Monday and Tuesday are on the right (in Hebrew, the order would be reversed to read right-to-left):

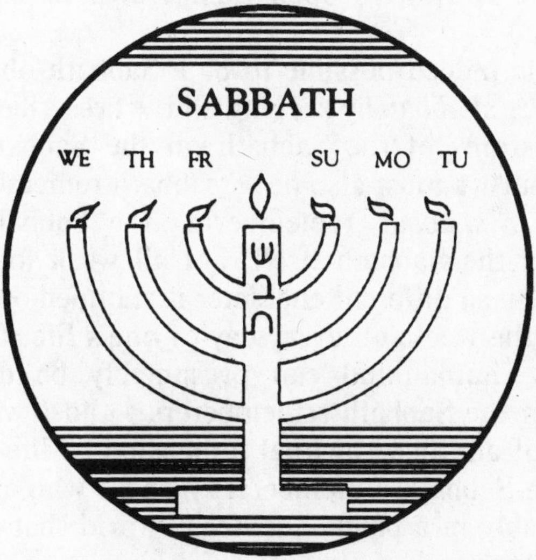

This graphic description is grounded in an ancient interpretation of the two-fold opening word of the Sabbath commandment in the Decalogue: *zachor* – "remember" the Sabbath, namely, hold on to its experience and remember it even three days after it is gone (Sunday, Monday, Tuesday); and *shamor* – "keep" the Sabbath, watch out for it even three days before it comes (Wednesday, Thursday, Friday). This idea is also reflected in *halakha* (religious law) concerning the Sabbath, as one is permitted to recite the *Havdalah* prayer, the parting blessing recited at the exit of the Sabbath, until and including the following Tuesday. The entire week takes its shape insofar as we can direct it towards the Sabbath, insofar as we let the days open to the Sabbath as flowers open their leaves to face the sun.

It is indeed possible to be a Sabbath observer, a *shomer shabbat*, by keeping all the prescribed laws and customs of the Sabbath on the Sabbath day itself, but we must also be a "sabbath rememberer," a *zocher shabbat*, remembering the Sabbath not only on the Sabbath itself, but all week long. By doing this, a different character is stamped on every day of the week, on every day of one's life. Consequently, humankind can presumably be divided between the Sabbath rememberers – those who are aware of another, spiritual dimension of life – and the non-Sabbath rememberers – those who are lost irreparably in a profane material world that knows no Sabbath.

The entire week is a vestibule to the Sabbath for there is no celebration without preparation. More than any other day, however, Friday is the day on which we prepare ourselves to enter the Sabbath. How our Sabbath looks depends very much on how our Friday looks. From ancient times we have the following account of the six trumpet-blasts that were sounded on Friday afternoon in Jerusalem, the city of the holy Temple. According to the tradition preserved in detail by the school of Rabbi Ishmael:

Six blasts, they relate, were blown on the eve of the Sabbath. When the first was begun, those who stood in the fields ceased to hoe, plow, or do any work in the fields; and those near to town were not permitted to enter it, until those more distant arrived, so that they should all enter simultaneously. But the shops were still open and the shutters were still lying down (the shutters were placed on trestlets during the day to serve as slats).

When the second blast began, the shutters were removed and the shops closed. Yet hot [water] and pots still stood on the range.

When the third blast was begun, what was to be removed [for the evening meal] was removed and what was to be stored away [for the next day] was stored away, and the lamp was lit.

Then, there was an interval for as long as it takes to bake a small fish or to place a loaf in the oven, then a *teki'ah, teruah*, and a *teki'ah* [the three musical figures which are blown on Rosh Hashana] were sounded and one commenced the Sabbath.[115]

In our day too, it is customary all over Israel for shops, offices and factories to close on Friday at noon, in order to give people some time between affairs of the mundane world and the Sabbath.

On Friday afternoon, Rabbi Isaac Luria, the

Holy Ari, the Master of Kabbalah (1505-41) used to immerse himself in the ritual bath twice – once to wash off the mundane week, and a second time to take on the holy Sabbath. A free Friday afternoon is required to put things in order before the scheduled appearance of the Queen/ Bride. This is the time to finish the cooking, last-minute buying, washing and shaving, shoe polishing, and ironing.

> Everything must be in readiness before the Sabbath begins, so that no one need worry about buying a bottle of milk or sewing on a button, or paying a bill, or seeing a customer. Careful planning is required. The Seventh Day does not come prepackaged. One flick of a magic switch will not turn it on.[116]

The table, usually covered with a white tablecloth, is set before the arrival of the Sabbath; upon it are laid out the best cutlery and dishes, bottles of wine, fragrant flowers. Everything is ready for the kindling of the Sabbath lights which marks the official end of Friday and the solemn entrance of the Sabbath.

Perfection and Partnership

Many reasons are offered for the central place given to the kindling of the Sabbath lights (originally with oil and wicks, nowadays usually with candles).

Some of the reasons are practical (e.g., to avoid sitting in the dark, as one is not allowed to kindle fire on the Sabbath itself); some polemical (the argument with certain fundamentalist sects who interpreted the ban on kindling fire on the Sabbath[117] to mean that one cannot use fire in any form during the Sabbath); some mystical (as God began creation with the words: "Let there be light," so do we begin the celebration of creation with light); some poetical (the beautiful image of the candle-lighting usually done by the mother of the household which has inspired numerous artists; the quiet modest whisper of the candles which casts peace and silence all about). Whatever the reason, from the minute the Sabbath light is kindled – Sabbath is in. On kindling the lights, a blessing is recited on fulfilling the ritual:

> Blessed are Thou, Eternal, our God, Sovereign of the Universe, who sanctified us with His commandments and ordained us to kindle the light of the Sabbath.

The transfer from the profane to the sacred takes place not only in the change of mood or pace which comes with the lighting of the candles, it must also be pronounced in words. It is not until we express our feelings in words that they become crystallized and binding. The same phenomenon is known to us in the process of the repentance of sin, which requires, according to Jewish law, the act of verbal confession.[118] It is only with verbalization that feelings, sometimes vague and nebulous, take on precise substance. The same occurs on the Sabbath in the declaration which opens the Sabbath celebration and is known as *kiddush*, namely "sanctification." In the beginning it was only God who sanctified the seventh day, now it is also the human being who declares it holy. The *kiddush* includes a recital of Genesis 2, verses 1-3, in addition to a blessing over wine or bread and another blessing over the holiness of the day [*kedushat ha-yom*]. "Whoever recites the verses of *vayekhulu* [the heaven and earth were finished, etc. – the opening words of the *kiddush*] on the Sabbath," say the Rabbis in the Talmud, "it is as if he becomes a partner with the Holy One in the act of creation." The pronouncement in the *kiddush* is taken as evidence and one must therefore stand up while reciting it, just as a witness in court "takes the stand" while testifying.[119] The following is recited:

> And it was evening and it was morning: the Sixth Day. And Heaven and earth and all their host were completed; then, with the Seventh Day, God completed His work which He had made, and with the Seventh Day He ceased from all of His work which He had made. And God blessed the Seventh Day and made it holy, for with it He had ceased from all of His work which He, God, had brought into existence in order to continue the work of creation upon it.
>
> Blessed be You God, our God, King of the Universe, Who creates the fruit of the vine.
>
> Blessed be You God, our God, King of the Universe, Who has sanctified us by His commandments and taken pleasure in us, and in love and favor, has given us His holy Sabbath as an inheritance, the memorial of His work of the world's beginning. For it is this day which is first among all the days of holy convocation, a remembrance of the Exodus from *Mitzrayim*. For You have chosen us; You have sanctified us from among all peoples, and in love and favor have You given us Your holy Sabbath as an inheritance. Blessed be You God, Who sanctifies the Sabbath.
>
> Blessed be You God, our God, King of the Universe, Who causes the bread to grow forth from the earth.

Asserting God's creation of the world gives us a certain position vis-a-vis the world. It is a position of mutual acceptance of each other – of humanity and world.

Why is this evidence given over a cup of wine and/or a loaf of bread? Because those staple foods represent the substance of life and together with the oil used in the Sabbath lights mark a proper celebration of a universe created and blessed by God. The blessing promised to humanity if we live the righteous life is: "And... you shall gather your corn, your wine and your oil."[120] On the Sabbath, on every Sabbath, we attain this blessed perfection of the material world. Corn and wine (in the *kiddush* cup and/or loaves of bread) and oil (in the Sabbath lights) – three blessings that welcome the Sabbath and celebrate the creation as our ancestors did in the days of old when on the Sabbath they brought their offerings to God.[121]

To be sure, wine and bread in Jewish tradition are just that, wine and bread. They do not represent any mysterious symbolism. Wine is used when ushering in the Sabbath, because wine "gladdens one's heart"[122] and puts one in a joyous mood befitting the spirit of the Sabbath. Another reason offered is that both wine and bread clearly demonstrate the partnership of humanity and God in the act of creation. Neither wine nor bread grow on trees. It is God who created the vine and we who extract wine from it; God who makes the corn and wheat grow and we who make bread of them. Does not the last word in the story of creation which introduces us to the Sabbath – *la-asot*[123] – state that God created the universe for humanity to continue making it? What better way is there to celebrate creation than to partake in products which are the combined result of the creation of God and the handiwork of human beings?

Between Light and Fire

Sabbath begins in a cosmic setting. It first transpired when God created the world. It remains forever a glimpse of eternity within fleeting time; an encounter between the transcendent seventh dimension and the six material dimensions of this immanent world. Sabbath was meant to give us a concrete sense of the divine, an opportunity to experience the spiritual in the here-and-now of our corporeal existence. In no way does it mean to mix the two realms or to blur the differences between them. Sabbath does not come to raise up humanity to sacred heights and thereby obliterate the boundaries between the holy and the profane as some religions propose to do, but to underline both realms. Judaism sees the secret of human knowledge in discerning between things, even as they appear to us in their oneness.

The Sabbath is ordained by God Himself and is actually built into nature from its very beginning. It does not really matter what we are doing or where we are – as soon as the sun sets on the sixth day, Sabbath is here. Nevertheless Jewish tradition understood that if we wish to experience the Sabbath, we cannot simply "leap" into it without proper physical as well as mental preparation.

There is an act of *kiddush*, of "sanctification" of the day, enacted both by God and by us. The seventh day does not become Sabbath on its own, automatically; it requires a conscious transition from the secular to the sacred.

A similar transition is required at the exit of the Sabbath. Sabbath departs with sunset, but it does not leave us until we are ready to say the *havdalah*.

It surely is not easy to let Sabbath go. Who wants to leave behind this paradisical life of peace and tranquility and go out to face the storms and grim realities in the week ahead of us?

The *havdalah* ("separation") ceremony comes to remind us that Sabbath in this world must come to an end. As human beings we cannot yet afford to enjoy an unceasing Sabbath. That would make us forget the difference between light and dark, between holy and profane, freedom and slavery. Our being human before God obliges us to discern between Sabbath and the rest of the week; between a day in which we are overtaken by a gratifying feeling of being created and a week when we assume the responsibilities of being creators, or rather co-creators with God, in mending this world and bringing it somewhat closer to an ideal state of Sabbath.

We know now what Sabbath is. We were just given the chance to feel it and to taste of it. That is why we are longing for her return, knowing that the perfect Sabbath is not here yet, and that we have to wait and we have to work for her coming.

In order to be able to do so, we must draw a clear line between Sabbath and other weekdays, between the sacred and the profane, between light and darkness.

The Sabbath we have just experienced has reassured us that we are capable of partaking in genuine spirituality in this world; that even in our day-to-day life we can cultivate our potential to live a life of "reality plus," provided we let the rays of Sabbath filter through and reflect on the rest of the week.

This idea is an important ingredient of the *havdalah* ceremony at the end of the Sabbath.

Sabbath is short. It comes and goes within a span of twenty-four to twenty-five hours. Hassidic masters used to try to "prolong" the Sabbath deep into Saturday night. With all this – it is only one day against six. If you take each Sabbath, one at a time, it truly seems very short. But when adding up all the Sabbaths in an average life of seventy years, we find to our amazement that there are no less than *ten years of Sabbath* in our life. Not observing one Sabbath, one loses a day (or may even feel that it is gained, seemingly used for something "interesting" or "pressing" to do). Yet ignoring the Sabbath altogether one loses ten sabbatical years. Ten years which could have been devoted to spiritual and physical enjoyment; ten years of personal growth. A seventh part of a lifetime.

The *havdalah* makes us realize the place of the Sabbath in our lives.

It also helps us face bravely the fears which may fill us as we are entering a new week, not knowing what it has in store for us. The *havdalah* not only makes us see the next Sabbath which is awaiting us at the end of a week's tunnel, but also calls upon us to accept the week ahead of us as a welcome challenge to the spirit of creativity implanted within us by God Himself.

The main feature of the *havdalah* is the torch of fire over which a blessing is pronounced, acknowledging God as "Creator of the lights of fire." The fire created by God is handed over to us, to go on using it for another six days of creation in the task of shaping and perfecting the world.

The introduction of fire marked the beginning of civilization. Primitive humans worshipped fire. It provided warmth, food, light, tools and weapons; it enabled them to shape the world around them. They came to regard fire as an all-powerful god. Some people do so to this day, except that the fire-worshippers now use more sophisticated nomenclature, calling it energy or technology.

Torah and Jewish tradition also play much with fire. God's word comes to us in flames of fire.[124] A "perpetual fire" must burn on the altar,[125] and there are many similar instances in the Bible where the importance of fire is stressed. The Bible makes us realize, however, that while God may speak out of fire, fire is not God. While fire shapes things, it does not create them. God wants us to use fire and technology, not to be dominated and subordinated by them.

The world comes into being, according to the biblical story, with God solemnly pronouncing: "Let there be light." This first act of the creation of "light" likely includes the creation of all sources of energy. The creation of fire as such is not mentioned explicitly in this story. Rabbinic tradition fills in the gap.

Crowning the end of the biblical story of creation is the creation of Adam and Eve, as male and female. Soon after their coming into the world comes the first Sabbath. When the first Sabbath was over, Adam saw the sun go down for the first time and an ever-deepening gloom enfolded the created world. Adam's heart was filled with terror; Adam felt helplessly lost in the dark. God then took pity on Adam and endowed Adam with the intuition to take two stones and rub them against each other, and so discover fire, whereupon Adam gratefully exclaimed: "Blessed be the creator of the lights of fire."

This story stands in direct contrast to Greek mythology, which represents Prometheus as *stealing* fire from the jealous gods and secretly giving it to humanity, for which he is chained to a rock and tortured endlessly. In Jewish tradition, fire is not stolen, nor held back from humans; it is a heavenly gift to human beings to enable them to become partners with God in continuing to create the world and improve it.

The biblical story of creation is re-enacted every Sabbath in Jewish homes. The Sabbath is ushered in with a blessing over the lights, just as God in the beginning pronounced: "Let there be light." After six fiery days of creative work, God teaches us that a moment comes when all labor, even that of creation, must cease in order to make room for the life of the soul. We must remember that after the six days that were given to us "to do," we were given one more day "to be." Six days a week we are identified by what we do, one day by who we are, as we move from creation to creatureliness.

Sabbath enters with light and departs with fire. Sabbath itself was called a day of "joy and light." "No fire must be kindled on the Sabbath in all your dwellings."[126] The one exception is the "perpetual fire" on the altar, which must be kept aflame even on the Sabbath.[127] It is in the sanctuary where both the "eternal light"[128] and the "eternal fire" are kept.

Both light and fire are gifts from God and we need both of them. The right balance between the light of *hesed* ("grace") and the fire of *gebura* ("power"), between the fire of creativity and the light of the awareness that we are ourselves created and kept alive by God, is the secret of the good life in the eyes of the Torah. The positive precepts, all the "do's," were likened to light; the negative precepts, all the "don'ts," were likened to fire. Both together make one complete Torah.

Fire and its more modern transfiguration, technology, are there to serve humanity, not to enslave it. Misuse of fire is likely to destroy and bring the world back to chaos and *tohu*; the balanced use of light and fire which is perpetually maintained in the sanctuary of the Sabbath brings blessing, warmth and perfection.

We depart from the Sabbath not only with the torch of fire, but also with an awareness of our senses, all of which we are made to use during *havdalah.*

There are the fragrant spices, used as part of *havdalah* to help the soul overcome the agony of parting from the extra dimension (*neshamah yeterah*) with which it was endowed during the Sabbath. The soul does not partake of food or drink, but does enjoy good aromas.

There is the *havdalah* candle, over which we praise God for enabling us to enjoy the senses of touch and of sight.

There is the taste of wine, which again represents the combined effort of God who gave us the vine and humanity that made wine of it.

And above all, the *havdalah* acknowledges our God-given understanding to distinguish and discern between things sacred and profane, between light and darkness, between Israel and the nations, between Sabbath and weekdays. Such an understanding makes us human and helps us find direction and meaning in our life on this earth.

Each one of the acts performed during the *havdalah* ceremony is preceded with a *berakhah*, a blessing announcing the act. The *brakhot* are recited in a particular order, with the blessing over the wine first, followed by the blessings over the spices, the fire, and eventually the blessing discerning between the holy and the profane. This order was seen by Jewish mystics as representing a succession in the refinement of our senses, from the lower to the higher: the wine must be taken *into* one's mouth and tasted before one can enjoy it; the fragrance of the *besamim* (spices) could be sensed even when held *near* one's nostrils; the sight of the burning candle could be sensed even from *afar*, and the highest sense of all, the conceptual discerning taking place in the mind, could be applied to the abstract and utterly ephemeral. This elevating succession is reflected in the structure of the human face going upward from the mouth (tasting), to the nose (smelling), to the eyes (seeing), and eventually to the mind, which discerns spiritually and intellectually between good and bad, the holy and the profane, the rest of the week and the Sabbath.[129]

The Hidden Treasure

Thus we testify and declare in the *kiddush*: "And heaven and earth were finished and all there is within them...and God finished on the seventh day His work which He had done and He rested from all the work which He had done."

Did He really finish all His work? Does He not continue to be involved in His creation every minute of the time? The sages of the Talmud find here a lesson for us to learn when we come to emulate God in the observance of His and our Sabbath. He finished all His work, they say, daringly. He acted *as if* He finished all His work. Likewise, one should feel and act on the Sabbath *as if* all one's work is done. The verse comes to teach us that even in this secular world of ours, it is possible to stop the world, get off for twenty-five hours, and feel as if everything is taken care of and done. There is nothing that cannot wait. God Himself showed us that it is possible. In the *kiddush* we testify to this fact.

To stop every activity in no way means to stop

or still life but to enhance it. It means living intensely on a different, higher level. As a matter of fact, the only thing which can do away with Sabbath itself is life. When human life is in danger, all laws and restrictions of the Sabbath are suspended. The Sabbath was given for our sake and not vice versa. God's law was given to live by and not to stop life.

Moreover, not only should we not be concerned with things unfinished in the week gone by, we must not think or plan for the days ahead. The story is told in the Talmud about a pious person who was going on a walk on Sabbath afternoon; strolling past his vineyard he noticed that the fence around it was in need of mending. Immediately he made up his mind to attend to the job the day after the Sabbath. On second thought, however, it occurred to him that since the idea came to mind during the Sabbath, it would not be right to implement his plan. He left the fence unmended and was later rewarded as a treasure was discovered there.[130]

Who knows how many hidden treasures were lost to us because we did not leave ourselves any time free from concern about the past or planning the future? The constant awareness of the non-stop passage of time is one of the things that implants in us existential anxiety and dread of death. Only the Sabbath, the ability to construct an enclave of "special" time, "holy" time, eternal time-within-time, can give us the ability to transcend time with its pressures, its choking *angst* and dread. The Sabbath makes it possible for us to feel for a while "as if all your work is done" and that next week is another beginning, with yet another Sabbath shining at the end of the dark tunnel.

If we cannot see it this way, shall we not let our extra soul, the extra dimension of the holy and the "special" within us, see it? Shall we not give it a chance and invite the Sabbath to enter into our lives?

Appendix 1

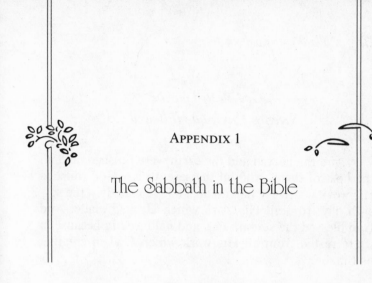

The Sabbath in the Bible

Biblical commentators frequently point out that the command to observe the Sabbath is repeated in the Bible *twelve* times, the most important being in the Decalogue.

The Sabbath is thus singled out in the Bible as the most important of all holy days. It is described not only as a memorial of Creation and of the Exodus from Egypt, but as the "sign of the covenant between God and Israel."

The biblical references to the Sabbath are either in the form of legislation such as the prophet Jeremiah's repeated pleas for Sabbath observance, or historical accounts such as Nehemiah's enforcement of Sabbath observance. All these references reveal the Sabbath as an old institution, generally recognized and widely honored, but still in a state of development, still far from the form it assumed in rabbinic times.

Although most of the details of Sabbath observance are post-biblical in origin, the general nature it was destined to assume, and the central role it was destined to play in Jewish life, are fully rooted in the Bible, as the following excerpts amply illustrate.

God Rested on the Seventh Day and Hallowed It

GENESIS 2:1–3

And the heaven and the earth were finished, and all the host of them. And on the seventh day God finished His work which He had made; and He rested on the seventh day from all His work which He had made. And God blessed the seventh day, and hallowed it; because in it He rested from all His work which God in creating had made.

The Fourth Commandment

EXODUS 20:8–11

Remember the sabbath day, to keep it holy. Six days shalt thou labor, and do all thy work; but the seventh day is a sabbath unto the Lord thy God, in it thou shalt not do any manner of work, thou, nor thy son, nor thy daughter, nor thy man-servant, nor thy maid-servant, nor thy cattle, nor the stranger that is within thy gates; for in six days the Lord made heaven and earth, the sea, and all that is in them and rested on the seventh day; wherefore the Lord blessed the sabbath day, and hallowed it.

DEUTERONOMY 5:12–15

Observe the sabbath day, to keep it holy, as the Lord thy God commanded thee. Six days shalt thou labor, and do all thy work; but the seventh day is a sabbath unto the Lord thy God; in it thou shalt not do any manner of work, thou nor thy son, nor thy daughter, nor thy man-servant, nor thy maid-servant, nor thine ox, nor thine ass, nor any of thy cattle, nor the stranger that is within thy gates, that thy man-servant, and thy maid-servant may rest as well as thou. And thou shalt remember that thou wast a servant in the land of Egypt, and the Lord thy God brought thee out thence by a mighty hand and by an outstretched arm; therefore the Lord thy God commanded thee to keep the sabbath day.

Food for the Sabbath Must Be Prepared on Friday

EXODUS 16:22–30

And it came to pass that on the sixth day they gathered twice as much bread (*manna*), two omers for each one; and all the rulers of the congregation came and told Moses. And he said unto them: "This is that which the Lord hath spoken: Tomorrow is a solemn rest, a holy sabbath unto the Lord. Bake that which ye will bake, and seethe that which ye will seethe; and all that remaineth over lay up for you to be kept until the morning." And they laid it up till the morning, as Moses bade; and it did not rot, neither was there any worm therein. And Moses said: "Eat that to-day; for to-day is a sabbath unto the Lord; to-day ye shall not find it in the field. Six days ye shall gather it; but on the seventh day is the sabbath, in it there shall be none." And it came to pass on the seventh day, that there went out some of the people to gather, and they found none. And the Lord said unto Moses: "How long refuse ye to keep My commandments and My laws? See that the Lord hath given you the sabbath; therefore He giveth you on the sixth day the bread of two days; abide ye every man in his place, let no man go out of his place on the seventh day." So the people rested on the seventh day.

The Sabbath, A Sign Between God and Israel

EXODUS 31:16–17

Wherefore the children of Israel shall keep the sabbath, to observe throughout their generations for a perpetual covenant. It is a sign between Me and the children of Israel for ever; for in six days the Lord made heaven and earth and on the seventh day He ceased from work and rested.

No Fire to Be Kindled on the Sabbath

EXODUS 35:1–3

And Moses assembled all the congregation of the children of Israel, and said unto them: "These are the words which the Lord hath commanded, that ye should do them. Six days shall work be done, but on the seventh day there shall be to you a holy day, a sabbath of solemn rest to the Lord; whosoever doeth any work therein shall be put to death. Ye shall kindle no fire throughout your habitations upon the sabbath day."

The Sabbath, A Day of Rest And of Holy Convocation

LEVITICUS 23:1–3

And the Lord spoke unto Moses, saying: Speak unto the children of Israel, and say unto them: The appointed seasons of the Lord, which ye shall proclaim to be holy convocations, even these are My appointed seasons. Six days shall work be done; but on the seventh day is a sabbath of solemn rest, a holy convocation; ye shall do no manner of work; it is a sabbath unto the Lord in all your dwellings.

The Reward of Honoring the Sabbath

ISAIAH 58:13–14

If thou turn away thy foot because of the sabbath,
From pursuing thy business on My holy day;
And call the sabbath a delight,
And the holy of the Lord honorable;
And shalt honor it, not doing thy wonted ways
Nor pursuing thy business, nor speaking thereof;
Then shalt thou delight thyself in the Lord,
And I will make thee to ride upon the high places of the earth;
And I will feed thee with the heritage of Jacob thy father;
For the mouth of the Lord hath spoken it.

The Sabbath, A Universal Day of Worship

ISAIAH 66:23

And it shall come to pass,
That from one new moon to another,
And from one sabbath to another,
Shall all flesh come to worship before Me,
Saith the Lord.

Jerusalem's Glory and Downfall Depend on the Hallowing of the Sabbath

JEREMIAH 17:24, 25, 27

And it shall come to pass if ye diligently hearken unto Me, saith the Lord, to bring in no burden through the gates of this city on the sabbath day, but to hallow the sabbath day, to do no work therein; then shall there enter in by the gates of this city kings and princes sitting upon the throne of David, riding in chariots and on horses, they, and their princes, the men of Judah, and the inhabitants of Jerusalem; and this city shall be inhabited for ever.

But if ye will not hearken unto Me to hallow the sabbath day, and not to bear a burden and enter in at the gates of Jerusalem on the sabbath day; then will I kindle a fire in the gates thereof, and it shall not be quenched.

Israel's Continued Profanation of the Sabbath

EZEKIEL 20:10–13, 17–22

So I caused them to go forth out of the land of Egypt, and brought them into wilderness. And I gave them My statutes, and taught them Mine ordinances, which if a man do, he shall live by them. Moreover also I gave them My sabbaths, to be a sign between Me and them, that they might know that I am the Lord that sanctifies them. But the house of Israel rebelled against Me in the wilderness; they walked not in My statutes, and they rejected Mine ordinances, which if a man do, he shall live by them, and My sabbaths they greatly profaned; then I said I would pour out My fury upon them in the wilderness, to consume them.... Nevertheless Mine eye spared them from destroying them, neither did I make a full end of them in the wilderness. And I said unto their children in the wilderness: Walk ye not in the statutes of your fathers, neither observe their ordinances, nor defile yourselves with their idols; I am the Lord your God; walk in My statutes, and keep Mine ordinances, and do them; and hallow My sabbaths, and they shall be a sign between Me and you, that ye may know that I am the Lord your God. But the children rebelled against Me; they walked not in My statutes, neither kept Mine ordinances to do them, which if a man do, he shall live by them; they profaned My sabbaths; then I said I would pour out My fury upon them, to spend My anger upon them in the wilderness. Nevertheless I withdrew My hand, and wrought for My name's sake, that it would not be profaned in the sight of the nations, in whose sight I brought them forth.

Nehemiah's Enforcement of Sabbath Observance

NEHEMIAH 13:15–22

In those days saw I in Judah some treading winepresses on the sabbath, and bringing in heaps of corn, and lading asses therewith, as also wine, grapes, and figs, and all manner of burdens, which they brought into Jerusalem on the sabbath day; and I forewarned them in the day wherein they sold victuals. There dwelt men of Tyre also therein, who brought in fish, and all manner of ware, and sold on the sabbath unto the children of Judah, and in Jerusalem. Then I contended with the nobles of Judah, and said unto them: "What evil thing is this that ye do, and profane the sabbath day? Did not your fathers thus, and did not our God bring all this evil upon us, and upon this city? Yet ye bring more wrath upon Israel by profaning this sabbath."

And it came to pass that, when the gates of Jerusalem began to be dark before the sabbath, I commanded that the doors should be shut, and commanded that they should not be opened till after the sabbath, and some of my servants set I over the gates, that there should no burden be brought in on the sabbath day. So the merchants and sellers of all kind of ware lodged without Jerusalem once or twice. Then I forewarned them, and said unto them: "Why lodge ye about the wall? If ye do so again, I will lay hands on you." From that time forth came they no more on the sabbath. And I commanded the Levites that they should purify themselves, and that they should come and keep the gates, to sanctify the sabbath day.

Appendix 2

Shabbat—A Key to Spiritual Renewal in Israel

Three Pictures

PICTURE NUMBER ONE

It is Shabbat morning. We see a street in a fashionable section in Jerusalem (or for that matter, in Tel Aviv or Netanya or Beersheba). It is unusually quiet. Shops are closed, a lonely car cruises by timidly in silence. Older, younger people, tallit-bags under their arms, walk in different directions, but to the same destination: the synagogue. There are a variety of synagogues in the neighborhood, large and small, Sephardi and Ashkenazi, representing all styles, customs and backgrounds. There are many children, heads covered with white hand-crocheted *kippot*, on their way to synagogue, too. Shabbat holiness fills the air. Stretch out your hand and you can touch it.

PICTURE NUMBER TWO

Same day, Herzliyah Beach (or for that matter, Bat Yam Beach, or Ashkelon, or the public parks in the north or the south of the country). Hundreds, perhaps thousands, of vehicles of all makes and types, coming and going. It is the day of the cafe houses, restaurants, ice-cream and popcorn vendors. Also of the emergency rooms in the hospitals whose weekly reports keep up Israel's grim record as a world champion in traffic accidents. The noise and chatter, coming mainly from countless transistor radios, will not subside until late in the afternoon.

PICTURE NUMBER THREE

Same day, an orthodox neighborhood in Jerusalem (or in Bnei Brak, Petah Tikvah or elsewhere). Hundreds of men in black garb and fur hats, notwithstanding the hot summer climate, waiting for every passing car on the nearby road to greet it with shouts of "*Shabbes, Shabbes*!" Very often the shouts warm up into stone throwing, rioting, police interference, name calling (one of the favorites: "Nazi!"), mutual accusations of violence and cruelty between police, non-observant and orthodox. Of course, all of these are Jews and would no doubt protest vehemently if anyone dared to exclude them from the "children of Israel" referred to in the verse "And the children of Israel shall keep the Shabbat to observe the Shabbat throughout their generations for a perpetual Covenant." To be sure, all of them see themselves within the ancient Covenant.

The above three pictures give but a few of the many varied faces of the Shabbat in present day Israel. There is one thing, though, that *all* scenes have in common (from the Shabbat at the Hasidic Court to the one in the leftist secular kibbutz): the Jewish Shabbat is an integral part of life in this country; it is an existential reality that one cannot forget, ignore, or escape. It was, I believe, the late Rav Kook who said that while *huz l'arez* (the Diaspora) is marked by the fact that there are *shomrei shabbat* (Shabbat observers) there, the land of Israel, on the other hand, is distinguished by the fact of having *m'halelei shabbat* (Shabbat desecrators). When his interlocutor looked up with surprise at the saintly rabbi, who was a great lover of Zion, hardly to be suspected of slandering the Land, the rabbi explained that both places, the Diaspora and *Erez Israel*, are distinguished by the exception to the prevalent rule: When one looks at the Diaspora, one notices the Shabbat observers here and there because, except for them, there is no presence of Shabbat. The reverse is true in the Land of Israel.

Shabbat and Tension

It is a fact that Shabbat is central in every aspect of life – legal, economic, social, religious, cultural and political – in Israel. Even one who desecrates the Shabbat does, in many other ways, mark and observe it. This is perhaps the source of the tension, which is sometimes destructive but more often creative, and which marks Shabbat in Israel. This tension is not limited to the legal-political aspect, as part of the ongoing clash between state and religion in contemporary Israel, nor did it start with the legislation or implementation of these or other Shabbat laws. Its roots strike much deeper and permeate the very core of the social-cultural make-up of Israel reborn, since the earliest days of the modern Return to Zion in recent generations.

The dilemma of being "torn away" or drifting away from the Shabbat, by social, cultural, or economic forces, that exists for Jews in the western countries of the Diaspora is significant only to a very limited measure (if at all) for the Jew in Israel. The Israeli is not faced with Sunday or any other day as a rival or substitute for Shabbat.

On the other hand, the Israeli is faced with the new, unprecedented situation of bearing full responsibility for personally and individually making or shaping his or her Shabbat. The traditional frameworks of the *shtetl, mellah*, and family have broken down; a new ethnic religious community (as has emerged in the United States, for instance) has not yet arisen in Israel (with a possible exception of the *datti*-"orthodox"-*kibbutz*) since the Jew in Israel has felt no pressing need for separate ethnic group identification and there has been no suitable religious leadership that knows how to offer traditional religious values in new vessels. In public life, the Israeli Jew must face the challenge of the Shabbat while assuming the responsibility facing Israelis in their personal attempts to come to terms with whatever can be salvaged from the Shabbat which was abandoned in an act of anti-religious protest and later was destroyed in their parental homes.

To these difficulties one has to add the fact that "religion," which includes, of course, the Shabbat, is governed in Israeli public life by political power structures and through legislation which appear (justly or unjustly) in the eyes of many Israelis as attempts of monopolistic coercion tactics by orthodox groups with vested interests which one "has" to fight off. The Shabbat thus often becomes the victim of the feuding "secular" and "religious" camps, with many people wondering whether the gains acquired by Shabbat legislation are not offset by the loss of appreciation for the lofty world which the Shabbat represents and which could so enrich Israel's spirit.

Remember, Observe, Do

Against this background of inner tension, on the one hand, and, on the other hand, a process of general alienation of the Israeli from traditional forms as well as from revolutionary values associated with the earlier generation of the "Founding Fathers" of Israeli society – one can distinguish certain interesting developments which are presently at work in the shaping of the Shabbat.

I should like to group these developments along the lines of the three-faceted understanding of the Shabbat as I read them in Scripture and as they are represented in much of the intricate Shabbat symbolism. These are: 1)*Zakhor* – remember the Shabbat Day, as in Exodus 20:8; 2)*Shamor* – observe, or keep, the Shabbat Day, as in Deuteronomy 5:12; 3) *La'asot* – to make the Shabbat, as in Deuteronomy 31:16 (compare Genesis 2:3).

Zakhor – "remember" – denotes the spirit of the

Shabbat, the so-called *aggadah*, or poetry which is Shabbat; the memory and the expectation; the song and the beauty, the delight of the
soul, Shabbat the *Kallah*, the lovely bride.

Shamor – "observe" – denotes the body of the day, the Law which gives substance to the Love, the "do's" and the "don'ts," Shabbat the *Malkhah*, the commanding queen.

La'asot – "to do" – denotes the human effort to join our own creative spark to that of God's Shabbat in order that out of this union will come forth the best of divinely-inspired, human spiritual creativeness.

Observing the contemporary Israeli scene of Shabbat, one would find, with all the drab problematic tension described above, much fascinating creative activity covering all three aspects of *zakhor, shamor* and *la'asot.* There is much probing and on-going search among many sensitive Israelis to rediscover the eternal light of the Shabbat, not only as a nostalgic relic of the past, but as a fresh source of spiritual nourishment in the present and the future. These do not lie in the realm of the ethereal or the theoretical, as they might outside the Land. In *Erez Israel*, Jewish thought must eventually be translated into concrete reality. It inevitably leads from *zakhor* to *shamor* via the path of *la'asot.*

The manifold creative efforts in Israel of the various kibbutz movements to keep the Shabbat, the attempts to shape new permanent molds of *shamor*, of Shabbat ritual which are not a passive continuation of the past, are a case in point.

Recently, Arye Ben-Gurion, of kibbutz Beth Hashitah in the Valley of Jezreel, who founded and manages the Inter-Kibbutz Festival Archives, collected and published scores of *Kabbalat Shabbat* programs from kibbutzim throughout the country. Together with these he published a programmatic anthology dealing with the question of what Shabbat can, and should, mean to the spiritual, cultural and social life of non-religious Jews who are dedicated to the building of free, consciously functioning and conscientious Jewish communities.

The common underlying features of this fascinating collection of experimental Shabbat ceremonies in so many non-religious kibbutzim all over the country is that, in spite of the differences between them, one senses in all of them the awe and joy of welcoming a day from the Jewish past. There is a yearning to appropriate the inner meaning of Jewish tradition, while not being bound to do so because of religious obedience; a desire to replicate the meeting of heaven and earth that Shabbat represents while realizing that the Jewish earth is not so much different from what it was to their fathers and that as the earth now is real so must heaven be real. This calls for an intense searching in the ancient sources to discover the secret of the "good life" as understood by Jewish tradition, which stands for the oneness of God and His creation, the unity of humanity and the meaningfulness of life in spite of its seeming absurdity.

There are many ways in which the kibbutzim try to "receive" the Shabbat, not just as an idea, but as a day which is both a "gift from heaven" and a living reality.

What meaning is there today for the age-hallowed lighting of candles as a way of ushering in the Shabbat? Is it but an outdated religious superstitious act? Would colorful flowers or the melodious playing of flutes be more meaningful as a way of "receiving" the Shabbat? Should Shabbat be received in the common dining room or in the privacy of the family? Should the children be part of the ceremony or should they be the sole active participants in it? And what about the liturgy? Should the old prayers – which are so poetically rich – be used and to what extent? How much and what kind of new liturgy should be included?

Every kibbutz tries to answer those and other questions in its own way. What is common, however, to almost all of the exemplary programs collected by Ben-Gurion is that they all strive towards some kind of stability, permanence, "institutionalized spontaneity" – what one would call, in the language of Jewish liturgy, a *nusah*, a permanent form.

Thus the traditional heavenly Shabbat is groping to find itself a new "earth" in Modern Israel.

This creative approach to the Shabbat is accompanied by serious attempts at a re-interpretation of the tradition. The "new" does not want to be, or to appear, as utterly new; it desires to find roots in the past, and thus what is taking place in this area in Israel surpasses its own boundaries and may have an enriching effect on the understanding of Judaism as a whole. Take, for instance, the interpretation of the Shabbat traditions suggested by the Israeli pioneering botanist, Noga Hareuveni, and how he brings together the heaven of Shabbat and the earth of Israel. The bounty of the earth as promised to the observers of the commandments of the Lord in Deuteronomy 11:14 is as follows: "I will give the rain of your land in its season...that thou mayest gather in thy corn, and thy wine and thine oil."

This earthly bounty was celebrated every Shabbat with the special Shabbat offering in the Temple that included fine flour mingled with oil and wine (see Numbers 28:9), as it is still celebrated every Shabbat in the Jewish home (transformed on Shabbat into a sanctuary) with the blessing over the lighting of candles (oil), the *kiddush* (wine) and the *challah* (bread of fine flour). How movingly beautiful the Shabbat in *Erez Israel* can be, if these are brought forth with your own hands from your own olive tree, your own field and your own vineyard.

Shabbat of Togetherness

Another interesting creative attempt "to do" the Shabbat that must be mentioned is that of *Shabbat Yahad*, a unique educational and cultural enterprise which was started eight years ago as a combined project of a group of Israelis and a group in Canada (Congregation Shaar Hashomayim in Montreal). The purpose of *Shabbat Yahad* was to utilize the day for a renewal of spiritual and ethical values in Israeli society as well as to bring together Jews from the Diaspora and Israel for mutual spiritual enrichment within a genuine, creative Shabbat experience.

The organizers of *Shabbat Yahad*, in summing up seven years of operation, saw it as a most successful "pilot project" which could spread and, eventually, become a popular pattern for the celebration of the Shabbat for many Israelis. *Shabbat Yahad* has, so far, attracted several hundred families representing all segments of Israeli society. While attempts to form communities in Israel on the basis of neighborhood proximity have not yet been very successful – because of the gap separating religious from non-religious, Sephardi from Ashkenazi, newcomers from veterans, left-wingers in political and social outlook from right-wingers – the Shabbat away from home and neighborhood in a relaxed atmosphere, open for spiritual and personal growth in togetherness, has given rise to a new type of nationwide community, which meets several times in a year. Each Shabbat is dedicated to intensive study and open debate at the feet of great scholars (condition: no publicity) on some vital issue of Israeli life in the light of the classical sources of Judaism. *Shabbat Yahad* participants (those who so desire) pray together in a relaxed, congenial atmosphere of fellowship and partake in the traditional Shabbat delight of good food, animated song and often dance together while enjoying the rare opportunity to speak their minds, to express ideas and dreams beyond what might be "expected" from the particular "labeled" status of each person. If Shabbat means freedom, the best place to practice and experience it under the Israeli style of life is away from home, among a community of people who gather together to celebrate it. Some of the ideas guiding *Shabbat Yahad* may not be new to Americans who are familiar with retreat and community experiences; they are, however, new to Israelis.

The idea of Shabbat as a means of a creative togetherness is now being emulated by many groups in Israel after the pattern set by *Shabbat Yahad*. The fact that such a Shabbat has a counterpart group outside of Israel that functions according to similar lines and carries over some of the creative ideas developed in *Shabbat Yahad* in Israel opens new vistas for Diaspora/Israeli combined efforts towards renewal, for which Shabbat is both philosophically and practically a most important key.

APPENDIX 3

Sabbath:

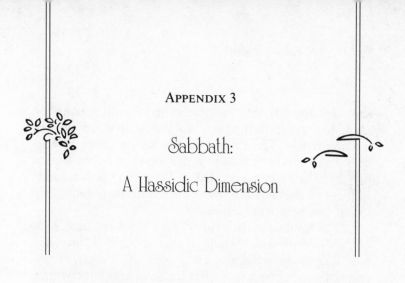

A Hassidic Dimension

The Sabbath is one of those precious heavenly gifts that are given again and again.

Many generations have been privileged to receive her as the wise and aged queen, and still to find her new, a radiant bride.

There is no end to the meanings discovered in the Sabbath in every generation; there is no limit to the secrets hidden within this enchanted "sanctuary in time." What Abraham Heschel did in our generation, in presenting us with *The Sabbath: Its Meaning for Modern Man*,[131] was not something that had never been done before. Even in the Torah itself, the Sabbath is revealed to us from one chapter to another in growing meaning: from a remembrance of Creation[132] to a mark of the Exodus,[133] and an everlasting sign between God and his people.[134] Sabbath is tied to the sanctuary in space[135] as well as to the holiness of the inner mystery of our personal being.[136] The Torah unfolds for us, as if by surprise, ever new ways of translating the command "to sanctify" the day into tangible expression, like confinement to a prescribed area,[137] or the prohibition against making fire.[138] The Prophets show us yet other aspects of Sabbath, in letting us into the secret of Sabbath as a delight. They emphasize that in order to experience the fullness of the Sabbath, we must refrain from indulging in any business transactions.[139]

The Rabbis, in their turn, find a thousand new faces of the Sabbath which smile in that enchanted, mysterious way from whatever angle you draw near. They encased the Sabbath in a solid frame of laws, thirty-nine *avot melakhah* ("categories of forbidden work"), countless *toladot* ("extensions [of forbidden work]") and *toladot* of *toladot*[140] – but at the same time they crowned her with the most tender garlands of love and poetry.

They whispered into our ears the secret of the "extra soul"[141] that joins us at the entrance of Sabbath in the luminous rays of sinking sun on Friday afternoon, and departs from us until the next week, regretfully, in the soft melodious shadows of the Sabbath twilight to vanish completely with the flame of the Havdalah candle. They opened our eyes to see the two angels walking at our side as we come home from the synagogue on Friday night[142] and enter our home, transformed into a palace, to greet members of our family, the mother queen, and the princes and princesses around the royal table. It was the Rabbis who illuminated our homes with the brightness of the Sabbath candles[143] and lit our hearts with the shining hopes of the imminent redemption of which the Sabbath is but a foretaste.[144] It was they who made us wash, change clothing, become different, outwardly as well as inwardly, upon entering the Sabbath.[145] Thus your dress on Sabbath should not be the same as your weekday apparel, your speech on Sabbath should not be as your speech during the week, your thoughts on Sabbath should not be as your thoughts during the week. On Sabbath you are another person, they convinced us, by sharing with us hundreds of minute detailed laws – laws which they hewed from the heavy granite of the mountains of *halakhah*, only to string them lightly on the golden hair of the one they called queen and bride in the *aggadah*. The laws of Sabbath, they said, are like mountains strung on one hair.[146]

Only God, Torah, Israel, the people, and the land of Israel could be given the same abundance of love and insight bestowed upon the Sabbath in talmudic and midrashic literature. Unable to express everything they wanted to say, the Rabbis resorted when describing the Sabbath to the epitaph, "a hidden treasure."[147] With all that can be spoken, more remains hidden, waiting to be unearthed in generations to come.

The medieval Jewish philosophers, poets and codifiers walked on the solid ground laid out for them by the Rabbis. The philosophers tried, as did the earlier philosophical apologetics,[148] to discover the logical virtues of the Sabbath, its benefits for the life of the faith, for the highest good of individual and society;[149] the poets filled the Sabbath eve and day with song and music which enhanced the structure of joyous observance established by the codifiers and expressed in the liturgy. The great tower of the Sabbath rose strong and tall by the turn of the first millennium. What more could be told that had not been told already? What more could be sung that had as yet not been sung in praise of the Sabbath? What remained to be done that was still not done to mark every hour and minute of the Sabbath, the beloved?

And yet in every age and every generation, the Sabbath is given over and over again. It was, surely, given to us again very powerfully in Jewish mysticism and the kabbalah. "It would be no exaggeration," says Gershom Scholem, "to call the Sabbath the day of the Kabbalah. On the Sabbath, the light of the upper world bursts into the profane world in which man lives during the six days of the week."[150] The kabbalah bathed the entire week in the light of Sabbath. And Sabbath itself? It becomes synonymous with the name of God, it is central to the mystic, mythical language created by the kabbalah, and it is crowned as the day when the masculine and feminine aspects of the Godhead are joined through divine nuptials in which mortals too can take part.[151]

The Sabbath of kabbalah is an integral part of the divine *sephirot*; it is sometimes identical with the *shekhinah.*[152] It moves in a celestial world, and we move with it. Every meal of the three (or four) meals of the Sabbath represents a different stage in the great divine wedding. Every move of ours here in this world explodes in erotic mystical symbolism, filling every minute of our Sabbath with an awesome, indescribable divine joy. We become active partners in a great cosmic drama.

The modern Hassidism of Israel Baal Shem Tov (1700-1760) was borne on the wings of the kabbalah.[153] It grew out of kabbalah and at the same time away from it to create its own world. It is said that, while kabbalah meant to raise us up to heaven, Hassidism lowered the heavens to us.[154] It made some of the esoteric principles of kabbalah accessible to large segments of the Jewish masses. It "domesticated" the kabbalah into the movement that translated its ideology into a rich way of life for the individual and the community.

It will, probably, remain debatable whether Hassidism deliberately undertook to "change" kabbalah or to "neutralize" it.[155] The changes were inevitable, though, because of the nature of Hassidism as a social movement. The Hassidic concept of Sabbath also changed; while Hassidism draws its teachings and inspiration about Sabbath from all the sources that preceded it, particularly the kabbalah, the Hassidic Sabbath is yet a new one, the revered queen transformed once again into a young, glowing bride. From a background crowded with customs and *Kawanoth*, it sprouts forward in new melodious song, in newly heralded harmony spun between the *zaddik* and his followers, between one Hassid and another.

One cannot describe the emergence and phenomenal growth of the Hassidic movement without the centrality of Sabbath, both as an idea and a lived event.

Sabbath was the meeting point between the Hassid and his mentor, the *zaddik*. The meals eaten together on Sabbath in the company of the *zaddik* and, no less important, other Hassidim, cemented the Hassidic fellowship, which is a cornerstone of the movement.

Early Hassidic literature, both of philosophical and popular types, is filled with references to the Sabbath. The trend has not ceased and has even increased in later Hassidic literature. Every generation of Hassidim, it might be stated, has offered us still a new face of Sabbath.

With the beginning of the nineteenth century, the Hassidic movement entered the second, triumphant stage of its history.[156] During the fifty years that passed from the death of its founder (1760), the movement spread far and wide, the secret of its rapid growth remaining a riddle up to this day. At the same time, it also branched out ideologically. While the root of all is one – Israel Baal Shem Tov – the branches differ greatly from each other. They represent a most variegated panorama of philosophies and emphases. By the end of the first decade of the nineteenth century, the greater part of the Jews of Eastern Europe (which was the majority of the Jewish people of the time) were "converted" to Hassidism.[157] Numerous *zaddikim*, each having his own unique personal style, "held court" in scores of towns and villages. The roads of Eastern Europe were filled with Hassidim traveling to their *rebbes.* The forests echoed with their songs, and the fires burned in wayside inns to warm elated groups of young and old men telling the wonders and citing the teachings of their masters, on their way to and from a Sabbath with their rebbe. (*Oif Shabbes,* that is the accepted Yiddish expression, that, although grammatically incorrect, took hold also in Hassidic Hebrew writings "*nosi'im al shabbat el ha'zaddik.*")

Political developments during those years – the failure of Napoleon's campaign in the East, the redivision of Poland – all helped put Hassidism on the map as a geographically divided movement, with clear distinguishing lines between one country and the other – between Ukrainian, Lithuanian, and Galician Hassidism, for example.[158] The regionally divided groups developed in many different ways. The struggles that had raged within the Jewish community between the Hassidim and their opponents, the *Mitnagdim,* for over fifty years subsided, to make room for another battle, this time against the *Maskilim,* representing the "enlightenment" movement, which spread from Germany eastward. This was a fierce battle that often found both Hassidim and Mitnagdim on the same side of the barricades, fighting the common enemy, who was in most cases supported by the government of the land, which would have preferred to "enlighten" its Jews and assimilate them rather than let them be influenced by the Jewish mystical "obscurantism" preached and practiced by the Hassidim.[159]

By this time there was already a growing Hassidic literature, consisting mainly of ideological and theoretical volumes authored by some of the founding fathers of the movement, but not including the Baal Shem Tov himself, who did not leave any written teachings. The struggle with the Maskilim and the developing literary taste of the contemporary Jew,[160] not excluding the Hassid, required a more massive and directed literary response, which indeed came about in the popular *Shivhei HaBesht* (*Legends of the Besht*), first published in 1815, in the more popularly directed epistles of Shneur Zalman of Ladi, and in the engrossing, though chaotic, writings of Rabbi Nachman of Bratzlav – all of them appearing in the Ukraine and Lithuania. In Galicia, which became a great center for Hassidism and one of the main forums of the Hassidic-*Haskalah* ("Enlightenment") struggle, there emerged at that time Rabbi Zvi Elimelech of Dinow, perhaps the most prolific of all Hassidic authors.

Rabbi Zvi Elimelech of Dinow

Rabbi Zvi Elimelech was fortunate in more than one way in becoming a classic Hassidic author. Born in 1783,[161] he lived at a time when Hassidism had already emerged as a definite socio-ideological movement in Judaism. He had a vast amount of written and oral material from which he could draw to write his own works and indeed Rabbi Zvi Elimelech's books are not outstanding for revolutionary or original ideas. Their importance lies in the fact that they constitute an authentic overall summary of the life and thought of Hassidism as a total expression, not confined to one or another of its more individualistic manifestations. Most of his twenty-nine published books rapidly became Hassidic classics for the entire movement, or for almost all of it.

Rabbi Zvi Elimelech was also fortunate in that he lived at a time when a very significant transformation took place within the Hassidic movement, namely, the transfer of leadership from master to disciple rather than from father to son, a phenomenon which was soon to become the rule in the various Hassidic dynasties.[162] Rabbi Zvi Elimelech was favored, too, in his association, first as disciple, and later as friend and colleague, with a very colorful and resourceful galaxy of Hassidic masters. His unassuming nature and born humility made it possible for him to learn much from all those he came in contact with. His three main masters were Rabbi Israel of Koznitz, Rabbi Mendeli of Rimanov, and Rabbi Yaakov Yitzchak, the famous "Seer of Lublin." All three were disciples of Rabbi Elimelech of Lyzansk, the author of *No'am Elimelech*, whose sister was the maternal grandmother of Rabbi Zvi Elimelech. The master of his masters he saw only once, when he was held in his arms at the age of four. He claimed, nevertheless, that he never forgot the look of this great-uncle of his, who was responsible for transplanting Hassidism to Poland and whose book *No'am Elimelech* was most likely an inspiration and model for Rabbi Zvi Elimelech's own books.[163]

He did not assume leadership as a *zaddik* in his own right until after the passing of his teachers. In the spring and summer of 1815, both Rabbi Mendeli of Rimanov and the Seer died, which gave rise to a large number of new hassidic courts that sprang up all over Galicia and Poland. Although all of the new masters were former disciples of the Seer, each went his own way and chose his own style. Most of them founded great Hassidic dynasties that have continued down to this day. Many established themselves as local rabbis of their communities, and thus served in the dual capacity of community rabbi, head of the local religious court, and also as rebbe, spiritual leader of a large number of their Hassidim, who traveled from near and far to sit at their feet.

This phenomenon marks an interesting change in the role of the Hassidic master outside of Poland, where the *zaddik* was not, or rarely was, identical with the local community rabbi. It shows the extent to which Hassidism had taken hold over Jewish life in those regions of Eastern Europe. It also added local community responsibilities to the spiritual concerns of the Hassidic master, who was now required to be grounded in the life of the entire community.

Such was the role of Rabbi Zvi Elimelech in the various towns in which he served as rabbi and rebbe simultaneously. We find no other reason for his frequent moves from one location to another except his desire to be in living contact with as many communities as possible. The amazing element in his story is that in his short lifetime – he lived only fifty-eight years[164] – he managed to produce such an impressive number of books, which deal with almost every possible subject in Jewish scholarship, from Bible and Mishnah commentaries, talmudic discourses, and legal responsa to Hassidic and moralistic homiletics and organizational programs.

He had a great message to impart. He held in his mind the accumulation of all that Hassidism had taught down to his time, and he seems to have been a compulsive writer. He thus became what one might call the Scribe of Hassidism in its peak period. Not only was he himself convinced of the immediacy and importance of his message, but so were his readers. Most of his books were published in many editions (*B'nai Issachar* and *Derech Pikudecha* both in eighteen editions, *Hasafot Maharza* in twelve, *Agra d'Pirka* in nine, and all others in at least two or three).[165] None of his books was published during his lifetime, although he had them edited and ready to print, as is evident in the cross-references from one book to another.

Hassidic tradition does not view authors of books very favorably. Hassidim believed in personal contact rather than the indirect touch of books, which is perhaps why a great number of Hassidic classics were published posthumously.

The first and most important author of early Hassidism was Rabbi Yaakov Yosef, who did more than any other person to perpetuate the original teachings of the Baal Shem Tov.[166] When the founder of the new movement passed away, Rabbi Yaakov Yosef expected to be chosen as his successor, but, as Hassidic tradition tells it, the *shekhinah* picked up her cane and bag and moved from Medzibuz (where the Besht lived), to Mezrich (where the great Magid, Reb Ber, lived), skipping over

Rabbi Yaakov Yosef. Of course, Hassidim assert, he was the closest disciple of the founder and was great in Torah and piety, but the *shekhinah*, they say, does not like authors...

This is also probably one of the reasons why Rabbi Zvi Elimelech did not found a large Hassidic dynasty, as his close friend the Belzer or his acquaintance Rabbi Israel of Rizhin did. He would not give up his writing for his career as a leader, and even while receiving people who came to him for his blessing or advice, he would continue writing while listening to their supplications. That practice made him popular with some of the women and plain folk. "We like him," they said. "He is a good rebbe because he writes down everything we tell him."

When one of those women asked him to look up her application for help, which he had written down in his book a few weeks earlier, he did not deny that all the trouble poor Jews and Jewesses poured into his ears were indeed well recorded in his books.

He also explained that he had become a writer reluctantly. One day, as he told it, when he was still very poor, he took hold of a small amount of money and sent his son to the store to get him some food. The boy came back with some sheets of paper instead. He sent the child again to tell the storekeeper about the unfortunate mistake, and this time the boy came back with an inkwell and pen. Every time the storekeeper was told one thing he heard something else; instead of food to eat Rabbi Zvi Elimelech ended up with ink, pen, and paper with which to write.[167]

And so he did. In his biography of Rabbi Zvi Elimelech, Rabbi Nathan Ortner lists twenty-nine published books and cites convincing evidence that many more were lost in manuscript.[168] His great-grandson, the Klauzenburger Rebbe in Netanya, testified that Rabbi Zvi Elimelech was such a fast writer that the ink on the top of a long sheet of paper was still wet when he had finished the last line on the page.[168] While waiting for the ink to dry, he would write a page for another book dealing with an altogether different subject, and then he would go back to the first one. His creative mind could move easily from one subject to another, with no noticeable damage done to either one.

His Writings: The Sabbath

As mentioned earlier, what gives his writings a special and central place in the by-now vast Hassidic literature is precisely the fact that he was not an individualistic innovator, but rather one who recorded and summarized the Hassidic thinking that had already become the heritage of hundreds of thousands of Jews in his time. His works could justly be entitled *Summa Hassidica*, as they draw from the sources of all of Hassidic literature. The library at his disposal, small but select, included, in addition to the Talmud and Midrashim, the Zohar and Ari writings as well as books by recent Hassidic masters (although he more often quoted them from oral tradition). There were also the books of the mystic philosopher Maharal of Prague, the homiletic classic *Olelot Ephrayim* by Ephraim of Luntschitz, and the Sephardic authors like Rabbi Moshe Alschekh; Rabbi Haim Ben Atar, author of *Or Hahayim* (who was very revered among Hassidim, including the Baal Shem Tov); and his contemporary, Rab Haim Yosef David Azulai (Hida, 1770-1840), the prolific writer and the world traveler for whom he seemed to have had a special liking and affinity.

And yet, without any deliberate attempt to be original, some of his personal views come through, revealing not only a scholar and theoretical moralist, but also a leader of his community, who responds intensely to the challenges of his own time and location. He sees himself, probably because of his writing ability, as the appointed spokesman of the Hassidic movement in Galicia. In this capacity he conducts a vehement ideological and literary warfare with the Maskilim, whom he accuses of trying to make inroads into the communities by disguising their true intentions, which would lead to Germanization of Jewish culture and eventual assimilation. He fights against any change in the style of life or dress which the "new winds" bring and try to introduce, and yet at the same time he is not cut off from reality.

Expounding on the importance of the warning laid down by the Rabbis, "Do not indulge in conversation with a woman,"[170] a principle that Hassidim preached and practiced, he shows that he is, nevertheless, fully aware of his own day. "In our times," he writes, "due to the heaviness of the exile and the hardship of making a living, the women engage in business, and talking to a woman is no longer an extraordinary event, but something we are used to. . . . I am writing this," he concludes, "to plead for the majority of our people and in particular Torah scholars, as I see so many of them are not meticulous regarding this matter, since it is impossible in our days."[171]

When his close friend, Rabbi Naftali of Ropshitz, got involved in a heavy quarrel with Rabbi Shlomo Leib of Lenchno and dispatched emissaries to ask Rabbi Zvi

Elimelech to join him in condemning Rabbi Shlomo Leib, the emissaries were very well received, but the reply they took back to their rebbe was a commentary on a passage from the portion of the Torah read that week in the synagogue: It is God Himself who asks Abraham to take Isaac, his son, and sacrifice him on the altar. Later, when the order is mitigated, it is an angel, not God, who calls to Abraham: Do not set your hand to the child and do no harm to him. Why does Abraham listen to the voice of the angel to undo what was commanded by God Himself? asks Rabbi Zvi Elimelech. It is to teach us that an angel takes precedence over God Himself when he says not to hurt a fellow Jew. "I do like and admire your rebbe, my friend Rabbi Naftali. I look upon him as upon a holy angel. Had you brought me a message not to hurt Rabbi Shlomo Leib, how I would have rejoiced to fulfill his wish. A message to hurt, however, that must come from God Himself."[172]

He is enraged by a certain rather common phenomenon of people who, under cover, or even in the name of religious fervor and exaggerated piety, are ready to commit crimes of defamation and character assassination against other people.

"A surprising thing I have seen here in our generation," he said (and remember that this was written more than one hundred years ago):

> Many self-righteous people are particularly meticulous in *chumroth* like *safek shatnez* ["not mixing materials in garments"], they refrain from eating meat which is not *glatt* or matzah boiled in water... [and] they believe that that makes them Hassidim... yet, at the same time, they do not refrain from defaming people whose height they can scarcely reach. They imagine they know how to distinguish between good and bad, between truth and falsehood.... Who gave them permission to transgress the explicit Torah prohibition of *loshon hara*,

> which is more severe than the three cardinal sins: idolatry, adultery, and murder. . . . The evil things they say about others demonstrate their own sins and evil passions that are inborn in them.[173]

All these writings reveal him as a man of courageous, nonconformist views, a man of his time, aware of what is going on around him and ready to take a stand on issues even though his views may not be popular. He sees his writing as a calling. Unlike most of the contemporary Hassidic books, his own are aimed at actual issues, imbued with a sense of clearly defined purpose: *Derech Pikudekha* tries to explain the way of the Hassid as giving new meaning to the observance of Mitzvot, and his *Mayan Ganim* calls for a counterattack of Hassidism against its aggressors of the Enlightenment movement. His major work, however, the one by which he is best known, is the *B'nai Issachar*,[174] a book which, according to its author's declaration, is designed to inject the holiness of time, something of Sabbath, into every day. Much before Samson Raphael Hirsch, who said that the calendar is the Jewish catechism,[175] or Abraham Joshua Heschel, who spoke about Judaism as a religion celebrating time rather than space,[176] Rabbi Zvi Elimelech sang his ode to time in writing this book. In it he tries to show how every day of the year could be illuminated by the light shining from the various sanctuaries of time that dot the Jewish calendar. At the top of all of the high points in time stands the holy Sabbath – the queen of all times.

The basic unit of time is the seven-day week. The Sabbath, according to the Zohar – which is perhaps the main foundation of Hassidic thinking – does not stand at the "weekend," nor even as the "week head" – but rather at the center of the week, like the central stem of a seven-branch menorah, with the three weekdays Wednesday-Thursday-Friday on its right, and the three days Sunday-Monday-Tuesday on its left [following the Hebrew order right-to-left], all drawing their sustenance from the center of the week, from Sabbath.[177] The first version of the Ten Commandments reads: זכור את־יום השבת לקדשו – "Remember the Sabbath day to keep it holy;"[178] the second version reads: שמור את־יום השבת לקדשו – "Observe the Sabbath day to keep it holy."[179] In the first half of the week, on Sunday, Monday, and Tuesday, we remember the Sabbath that has gone by, and on Wednesday, Thursday, and Friday we observe, look out, and wait for the Sabbath that is to come. It is only through Sabbath that we can survive the week looming between the Two Sabbaths.

The Sabbath, as she is portrayed in Rabbi Zvi Elimelech's *B'nai Issachar*, is the product of centuries of Jewish experience, a child of love and reverence. It is, above all, the day that gives one strength to go on living, to fill life with joy, with light.

He writes about the Sabbath as though of a beloved one.[180] While drawing heavily from the vast *aggadic* literature, the mystical book of the Zohar, and earlier Hassidic literature, he does at the same time express a strong personal, feverish attachment to his subject, standing before the day in love and awe. The often-quoted saying of the Zohar[181] in Hassidic literature, that *Shabbat* is one of the Names of God, plays a central role in his thinking. One does not use God's Name easily, "and I know of those who are meticulous in their behavior, that they are very careful not to utter the word *Shabbat* needlessly. And it is correct to do so."[182] Just as there are unclean places where one is not allowed to read from the Torah, so one is not permitted to pronounce the word *Shabbat* in those places.[183]

The conviction that *Shabbat* stands for the Holy Name, or the presence of God, sparks off a long series of commentaries using a variety of homiletical methods typical of allegorical and mystic literature. Rabbi Zvi Elimelech is a virtuoso in his use of those highly theoretical methods, eluding the danger of losing the central idea in the maze of endless speculations, such as *Gematria* (playing with the numerical value of the letters of the Hebrew root of a word). While perfectly adept in this methodology, he cleaves tenaciously to the central cords of the idea he pursues. To cite just a few examples:

Sabbath in the Zohar represents the Name of God. By Name, we refer to the appearance of the Transcendental God in this world. This was made possible through the act of Creation. The raw material which God used in creating this world of matter, according to one Zoharic theory greatly developed in Hassidic literature,[184] was contained in the twenty-seven letters of the Hebrew alphabet, each letter embodying a Divine spark which grants existence to the material world. The numerical value of the most known name of God, Y-H-W-H, is twenty-six; in creation God Y-H-W-H (twenty-six) projected Himself twenty-seven times through each one of the twenty-seven letters of the alphabet, in order to make this world possible. Now, 27 x 26 amounts to 702, which is, of course, the same numerical value as *Sh-B-T* (=702). Thus, *Shabbat* is God's name as it appears in this created world.[185]

By the same token, Sabbath represents perfectness. In Jewish mysticism the world is seen as broken and fragmented. It is "in exile" in no less than three dimensions: in space, time, and soul. The human soul is split, and parts of it are destined to bitter exile except on Sabbath, when the exiled splinters of the human personality can be gathered together in peace. There is also a terrible chasm separating man from woman, a rift which threatens the peaceful, fulfilled existence of human beings from the first moment following the creation of Eve, when Adam asserted in great shock: "This is now bone of my bones and flesh of my flesh."[186] Looking at Eve, Adam saw himself split in two as *etzem* ("bone") and as *basar* ("flesh"), interpreted in mystical allegory as representing the two dimensions of severity and grace between which a person is suspended constantly in tension. It is only on Sabbath that the two can harmonize, and one can find peace of mind and soul. This idea, which is derived, as Rabbi Zvi Elimelech proves, from the concept of Sabbath as a day of harmony and perfection, is, of course, inherent in the numerical value of *Sh-B-T* – a perfect combination of *etzem* (200) plus *basar* (502), which together equal Sabbath's numerical value (702).[187]

Of the three Patriarchs, Jacob was the one who succeeded in harmonizing the two opposing divine trends inherent in Creation (Jacob is represented in mystical allegory as the embodiment of the mediating *sephirah* of *tiferet*). After marrying Leah he worked for seven more years to earn the hand of Rachel. In seven years there is one full year of Sabbath days. A year of Sabbath made Jacob ready to unite with both Leah and Rachel, symbolizing again the two faces of Creation represented earlier by the dual facets of Eve.

In addition to his frequent use of *Gematria*, Rabbi

Zvi Elimelech ingeniously employs many other hermeneutical devices to develop his theory about the special place of Sabbath in the world of both God and people, and of the interaction between the two.

Thus he takes out of context the text of a well-known Mishnah, recited on Friday night, to give it a startling interpretation. The Mishnah reads: "Three things must a man say within his house when darkness is falling on the eve of Sabbath: 'Have ye tithed?' 'Have ye prepared the Eruv?' and 'Light the lamp.'"[188]

Rabbi Zvi Elimelech, in his homiletical commentary, sees in the Mishnah a mystical injunction to humanity on the eve of the Sabbath, when we are about to part from the darkness and enter into light of Sabbath. We are at that time enjoined to say three things in our home, meaning in our inner recesses – namely: *Isertam* (from *eser* = "ten") – have we made room in our soul for the ten *sephirot*, the ten emanations of Godliness? *Eravtam* (from *arav* = "to mix") – have we succeeded in mixing together the two dimensions of the Divine: *ahavah* ("love") and *yir'ah* ("reverence")? And lastly, have we kindled the inner light that comes with the Shabbat?[189]

Rabbi Zvi Elimelech has much to say about the association of Sabbath and light. He expounds elaborately on the rabbinic comment on the verse "And God blessed the seventh day"[190] – with what did He bless the day? With light. Blessing and light always go together in the same way as curse and darkness go together, as is proven in Job 3:4-9. This is why Sabbath is ushered in by lighting candles. Lights of Sabbath also represent Torah[191] and the soul of humanity. On Sabbath the three – Sabbath, Torah and Soul – join. Sabbath is thus the day of Torah,[192] a day when one is much more qualified to reach new depths of meaning in Torah, illuminated by the light which has been hidden until the coming of the Messiah but meanwhile shines through only on the Sabbath.[193]

This concept of Sabbath, although leaning heavily on kabbalah, receives special emphasis in Hassidic circles. This is probably because of the unique place the Sabbath occupied in Hassidic life, as the day when the Hassid came in contact with the *zaddik* to listen to the new light the master would shed on the Torah. The Sabbath is thus described, following the Zohar, as the quintessence of Torah.[194] But Rabbi Zvi Elimelech goes further in exploring its meaning.

Sabbath, he contends, is not only a day of extra clarity in grasping the meaning of Torah, but it is the form-giving element in material Creation. Without it all of Creation would be like a body without a soul. Leaving behind the Aristotelian terminology of form and matter, he goes on to say that Sabbath is the soul of the created world. Without it, as without the name of God, the world would not be able to hold together.[195]

Following now the central idea of Hassidism, that of *Dvekut*, or cleaving to God, Sabbath becomes the aim of life, allowing Rabbi Zvi Elimelech to offer a daring comment on the verb *kds* ("to make holy"), which is applied to the Sabbath both as an act of God[196] and a commandment to humanity.[197] In the sprit of the erotic symbolism of the kabbalah, he interprets *kds* in the sense of *kiddushin*, "consecration through marriage." God blessed the seventh day, He endowed it with grace, with light and harmony, and consecrated it; it can be said in a sense that He married the seventh day as a mate.

Human beings, on the other hand, are commanded to remember or keep the seventh day – to consecrate the day as in marriage, to develop an intimate relationship with it, "as man and woman do."[198] Rabbi Zvi Elimelech bases this interpretation not only on his enormous overwhelming feeling of love for the Sabbath, but also on the Midrash that tells how Sabbath came in front of God to complain: "To every day of the week you gave a partner. Sunday goes with Monday, Tuesday with Wednesday, Thursday with Friday, and only I am left without a mate." And God, blessed be He, replied: "The community of Israel will be your mate."[199] What to the rabbis of the Midrash was a metaphor of speech is reality for Rabbi Zvi Elimelech. Sabbath is celebrated in kabbalah as the day of the holy communion between the masculine and feminine *sephirot*;[200] it is also the day when husband and wife are commanded to be joined sexually.[201]

Hassidism attempted to bring God into this world, and claimed that not only the heavens but also the earth is the Lord's. Rabbi Zvi Elimelech, as one of the great exponents of Hassidism, has therefore much to say about the divine meaning that can be instilled in seemingly earthly activities, such as eating or cohabiting. The celebration of Sabbath through bodily delight is the best example of the possibilities by which humanity can express its worship of God through earthly and this-wordly things.

Rabbi Zvi Elimelech deals at length with the various aspects of delight expressed in the joy of Sabbath and reflected in its liturgy. A delight can no longer be felt if it constantly continues on the same level.[201] The delight of Sabbath increases from one step to the next. The process is expressed in the Sabbath liturgy, which changes from one service to the other, from Friday night, which represents the act of consecration in marriage, to Sabbath morning, when the lover showers gifts upon his beloved, culminating in the Sabbath afternoon service, the moment of intimate union of the lovers.[203]

The liturgy of the day, familiar to every Jew, serves for Rabbi Zvi Elimelech as a natural springboard for many of his ideas, as do the special additions introduced or practiced by the Hassidim. Why do Hassidim recite the Twenty-third Psalm ("The Lord is my shepherd") during the "third meal" of late Sabbath afternoon? he asks. There are, he replies, many kabbalistic explanations for this custom. Rabbi Zvi Elimelech's own answer is simple yet profound. The twilight of Sabbath afternoon is considered in the Midrash to be an hour of sadness, since Moses, the "trustworthy shepherd," passed away on Sabbath at that time of the day.[204] We therefore read the Twenty-third Psalm in order to comfort ourselves in declaring that although the faithful shepherd and great teacher left us, God is still our shepherd and we shall not want.[205]

And why is it the custom to eat fish at Sabbath meals? The answer to this question is also hidden in the very same psalm, verse six, *bin'ot deshah yarbitzayni.* D-SH-A is an abbreviation for *Dagim* ("fish"), *Shabbat* ("Sabbath"), and *Adam* ("humanity") – the only three elements in the story of Creation which were singled out for a special blessing by God.[206] Human beings eating fish on Sabbath represents all the parts of this triple blessing.[207]

He continues to emphasize that the delight enjoyed on Sabbath is not to be mistaken as an indulgence in worldly pleasures. The Rabbis word their sayings carefully: "whoever delights in the Sabbath,"[208] not in self-delight. The purpose of the day is to partake in the delight that is part of the essence of the Sabbath, a transcendental being coming to this world to be welcomed with spiritual yearning as well as with material rejoicing.

Sabbath comes once a week, as part of a cosmic happening. It is not up to us – as with the holidays – to pronounce its coming or to fix it on another day.[209] But it remains our responsibility to bring a glimpse of Sabbath into our day-to-day life. Hassidism stresses the importance of *hitbodedut* ("self-isolation") and advises every person to set aside some time during the day to be with himself. "A person who does not have at least one hour a day to be secluded with himself is no person at all" is a widely accepted Hassidic maxim.

In this spirit, Rabbi Zvi Elimelech demands that "every person – businessman or craftsman – set aside one hour a day in which he draws from the sanctity of Sabbath."[210] In this way the flight of time can be held and given meaning. We can infuse the temporal world with eternity, and raise ourselves to the heights of Sabbath each day of the week.

Notes

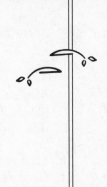

1. Jerusalem Talmud (TJ), tractate Berachot (Ber.) 1:5.
2. Isaiah (Is.) 56:2.
3. End of Hilkhot Shabbat 30:5.
4. Achad Ha'am (1856-1926), *Al Parashat Derakhim*, Vol. 3, ch. 30. For the central role played by the Sabbath in the history of Jewish survival compare Jehuda Halevi (1075-1141), *The Kuzari*, part 3, section 9-10; and also Emil Fackenheim, *Encounters Between Judaism and Modern Philosophy*, New York, 1973, pp. 107-108.
5. Exodus (Ex.) 31:16.
6. Leviticus (Lev.) 19:3; 19:30.
7. "Sabbath," as with the transliterations of many other Hebrew words, reached Western languages via the Greek translations of the Bible in a distorted pronunciation and spelling because of the lack of proper Greek letters for transliterating Hebrew syllables (i.e. *Avraham*=Abraham, *Shmuel*=Samuel, etc.).
8. For a compilation of the places in the Hebrew Bible dealing with the Sabbath, see Appendix 1.
9. *Tanna* (plural, *Tanna'im*) refers to the early sages of the Oral Law, whose opinions comprise the

Mishnah, Tosephta and Halakhic Midrashim (*Mekhilta, Sifra, Sifrei*, etc.) They lived in Palestine during the first three centuries of the common era.

10. Mishnah (M.) Hagiga 1:8.
11. Genesis (Gen.) 2:1-3.
12. Deuteronomy (Deut.) 32:4.
13. *Sifrei*, Deut. 32, 307.
14. Gen. 1:31.
15. Gen. 1:31-2:3.
16. It is interesting that both in Hebrew and in English there is a dual, even complementary, meaning to the word "end," both as "finish" and as "destination," or "purpose." Thus Abravanel (1460-1523) in his famous Bible commentary interprets the word *vayekhulu* in Genesis 2:1, not only in the sense that the heaven and the earth were finished, but also that they were brought to their destination, which is the Sabbath. Following this interpretation one is to understand the phrase in the Friday night liturgy which refers to the Sabbath as *tahlit shamayim va'aretz*, "the end of heaven and earth," in both connotations of "end." (See Hertz, *The Authorized Daily Prayer Book*, rev. ed. (New York: Bloch Publ. Co.), 1975, p. 378. See also Jerusalem Targum, quoted in *Torah Shleima*, Gen. 2:2).
17. Another explanation for the word *vayekhulu* is that it derives from the root kh-l-h as in Psalms 84:3, where it means "longing" and "yearning." Hence the expression in the liturgy of Sabbath morning (Hertz, p. 458), *hemdat yamim oto karata*, "Thou didst call it desirable of days."
18. This is yet another explanation for the word

vayekhulu, the opening word of the Sabbath passage in the Bible, based on the assumption that the word comes from *kli*, a "vessel." With the appearance of the Sabbath, heaven and earth turned into a "vessel" ready to receive the blessing and holiness given by God (Midrash, comp. *Sfat Emet*, and N.H. Tur-Sinai, *P'shuto shel Mikra, ad loc*).

19. Ex. 31:17.
20. Thus the word *vayinafash* referring to the Sabbath in Ex. 31:17 is interpreted to mean that on the seventh day God gave the world a soul, a *nefesh*.
21. See *Commentary to Genesis* by M.D. Cassutto, Jerusalem, 1972. Also N. Sarna, *Understanding Genesis*, New York, 1965, and Y.M. Grintz, *The Uniqueness of Genesis*, Jerusalem, 1983.
22. Ex. 20:8-11.
23. Gen. 2:3.
24. Ex. 20:8; Deut. 5:12.
25. Holy Sabbath would be translated in Hebrew *shabbat kadosh* or *kedoshah* not *shabbat kodesh*. The same applies to *ruah hakodesh*, which should not be rendered "holy Spirit," but rather "spirit of holiness." Also *erez hakodesh* or *ir hakodesh* which should not be "holy land" or "holy city," but land and city of holiness. Often *kodesh* stands for the Temple, or the site of the Temple in Jerusalem, as in Ex. 28:29, 29:6; Lev. 5:16; Num. 18:5; Jer. 25:30, 51:51; Ps. 63:3; and many others.
26. Ex. 31:14, Ezekiel (Ez.) 20:13; Nehemiah (Neh.) 13:18.
27. For numerous etymological explanations and proto-Semitic derivations of the root *kds*, see various biblical dictionaries. For a treatment of the

idea of the Holy, see Rudolf Otto, *Das Heilige* (English, *The Idea of the Holy*); J.S. Licht, *Encyclopedia Biblica* (Heb.), Jerusalem, vol. 7, pp. 44-62.

28. Mircea Eliade, *The Sacred and the Profane, the Nature of Religion*, trans. from the French by W.R. Trask. Eliade deals with the subject also in most of his many other books, esp. his comprehensive *A History of Religious Ideas.*
29. Lev. 19:2.
30. Sifra, Lev. 19:2. Comp. S. Hugo Bergman, *Kiddush hashem*, in *Bamishol* (Heb.), Tel Aviv, 1976, pp. 182-192.
31. On *Sefer Yezirah*, see Gershom Scholem, *Kabalah*, Jerusalem, 1974, pp. 23-31. See also Scholem, *Major Trends in Jewish Mysticism*, p. 69f.
32. Gen. 3:17-19.
33. In his thorough study on the "Origin of the Sabbath" (*Halashon Vehasefer, Emunoth Vedeoth* (Heb.), pp. 205-228), Prof. N.H. Tur-Sinai refutes all the "evidence" for the non-Hebrew origin of the Sabbath or the seven-day week. Comp. Solomon Goldman, *The Ten Commandments*, Chicago, 1963, pp. 160-167.
34. This was the view held by Jehuda Ha-Levi, see *Kuzari* 2:26, and now also verified by modern research, see *Encyclopedia Biblica* (Heb.), vol. 7, pp. 511-517.
35. John L. McKenzie, *A Theology of the Old Testament*, 1974, pp. 81-84.
36. Ibid, p. 83.
37. Martin Buber in *Moses*, p. 82.
38. Ex. 31:13-17.

39. *Pirkei d'R. Eliezer*, Ch. 3.
40. *Sof ma'aseh b'mahashavah tehilah* in the famous Sabbath poem by Solomon Alkabetz (1505-1576) – *Lekhah Dodi*, now part of the Friday night liturgy in all Jewish communities.
41. *Tahlit shamayim va'aretz*, Hertz (p. 379) translates as "the end of the creation of heaven and earth." See above note 16. See also Mayer Gruber, "Atta Kidashta," *Conservative Judaism*, vol. XIV, no. 4.
42. See the commentary of Ovadia Sforno (1470-1550) on Gen. 1:31.
43. *Hidushei Aggadoth Maharsha* (Samuel Edelis, 1555-1634) on Babylonian Talmud (TB), Tractate Aboda Zara 3; compare also Franz Rosenzweig, *Star of Redemption*, and A.H. Rabinavitz, *Olam Echad*, Jerusalem, 1976, p. 106.
44. Gen. 2:1-2.
45. Midrash Gen. Rabbah 2:10.
46. Gen. 6:5-7.
47. Midrash Gen. Rabbah 27:4.
48. *Seder Rabbah D'Breshit* 15:15, quoted in A. Bar-Tanna, *Pirkei Breshit B'Machsevet Israel*, 1973, p. 126. Compare *Sefer Hashabat*, ed. by Y.L. Barukh, Tel Aviv, 1963, p. 32. A particularly beautiful description of the world appears in *Sheiltot D'R. Ahai Gaon*, ch. 1.
49. *Pirkei d'R. Eliezer*, ch. 18.
50. Zechariah (Zech.) 14:7.
51. Gen. 2:3.
52. See Samson Raphael Hirsch, Commentary on Gen. 2:3.
53. Franz Rosenzweig, *Star of Redemption.* The idea of this trio and its correspondence to the three

prayers of the Sabbath Liturgy – Creation on Friday night, Revelation in the morning service, and Redemption in the afternoon – is first enunciated by R. Jacob b. Asher (1270-1343), in his *Sefer Haturim, Orach Haim*, section 292. One wonders if Rosenzweig knew the earlier source, or arrived at it through his own ingenious intuition. Rosenzweig, who lived from 1886-1929, was, according to Emil Fackenheim, the greatest Jewish philosopher of the modern era.

54. As to the history of the *Magen David*, the six-pointed "star of David" as a Jewish symbol, see G. Scholem, *Kabbalah*, Jerusalem, 1976, pp. 3-8.
55. Gen. 2:1-4.
56. See Zech. 14:9.
57. Ex. 16:23-26.
58. Buber, *Moses*, p. 80.
59. Ex. 16:23; 20:10; 35:2.
60. Ex. 31:14.
61. Gen. 2:3.
62. Ex. 20:8.
63. Ex. 16:29-30.
64. Ex. 35:3.
65. Ex. 16:23.
66. Num. 15:32-36.
67. Ex. 16:29.
68. Ex. 34:21.
69. Jeremiah (Jer.) 17:21-27.
70. Is. 58:13.
71. Neh. 13:15-22.
72. Jewish Chronicle Publications, 1961.
73. Ex. 31:13-17.
74. Mishnah Shabbat (Shab.) 7:2.

75. Neuwirt, *Shmirat Shabbat Ke'hilkhata*, Jerusalem, 1965.
76. Ex. 20:9. Several attempts were made in the course of the generations to classify and sub-divide the thirty-nine *avot melakhah* prohibited on the Shabbat. In explaining why the Mishnah lists "baking" rather than the broader "cooking," the Gemara responds that the first eleven *melakhot* reflect the process of baking bread (*siddura d'pat*). The next thirteen *melakhot* (12-24) reflect the process of preparing wool. The remainder of the list has been divided in various ways. The *Talmudic Encyclopedia* defines numbers 25-33 as part of the writing process; numbers 36-37 as *melakhot* connected with fire; number 38 as a separate category defined as "work completion;" and number 39 as a *melakhah* concerned with space rather than matter. Rabbi Gedalia Felder (*Yesodei Yeshurun*) lists the divisions in his introductory remarks from the order in which he treats the *melakhot* in the remainder of his book.
77. Philo Judaeus, c. 20 BCE – 50 CE, one of the earliest Jewish philosophers.
78. Midrash, S. Hashabbat, p. 28.
79. Samson Raphael Hirsch, *Judaism Eternal*, pp. 21-23.
80. *Mekhilta d'Rabbi S. Bar Yochai*, Ex. 20:9. On the value of labor in Judaism see the beautiful compilation of Rabbinic materials on the subject by my teacher, Dr. B.M. Levine, z.l., named *Masekhet Poalim*, Jerusalem, 1943.
81. *Muktzeh*,"set aside" or "excluded," is the term used in *halakhic* literature for all those items,

which by themselves do not cause violation of Sabbath, but were prohibited because they simply "do not belong" to the Sabbath. There are, according to Grunfeld, several different types of *Muktzeh*: a. Objects which, when Sabbath commenced, were inaccessible to use (e.g., fruit fallen from a tree on Sabbath, eggs laid on Sabbath); b. objects which can never be brought into use on Sabbath without transgressing the Sabbath law (e.g., animals, a lamp, money); c. objects whose normal use is for *melakhah* purpose (e.g., tools – these may not be handled for their own sake, as to show them to a friend, but they may be used for a purpose not involving a *melakhah* and they may also be moved if they are in one's way).

82. Amos 8:4-6.
83. TB Betza 16.
84. Neh. 13:15-22.
85. Ex. 34:21.
86. The Jewish mystical tradition of the *Kabbalah* also has much to offer in its own way to interpret this variant reading. While *zachor* would represent the masculine element, *shamor* stands for the feminine. On the Sabbath the great unification occurs. See G. Scholem, *On the Kabbalah and Its Symbolism*, pp. 139-140, and Y. Tishbi, *Mishnot Ha-Zohar* (Heb.), vol. II, pp. 412-440.
87. Psalms (Ps.) 62:12.
88. TB Shavuot 20.
89. Deut. 5:14.
90. Lev. 19:18.
91. Is. 58:13-14.
92. Midrash, Proverbs (Prov.) 31.

93. One is not to recite the regular weekday *Amida* on the Sabbath, because it brings to mind our material shortcomings which should not be remembered on the Sabbath. In Halakhic Literature (*Shulchan Aruch*, 288), there is a discussion whether one is allowed to cry on Sabbath. The ruling is against crying, except for those people for whom crying is a relief, even a delight.
94. Midrash Ex. Rabbah, 1:28: "He [Moses] saw that they had no rest, so he went to Pharaoh and said: 'If one has a slave and he does not give him rest one day in the week he dies, similarly, if thou will not give thy slaves one day in the week rest, they will die.' Pharaoh replied: 'Go and do with them as thou sayest.' Thereupon Moses ordained for them the Sabbath day for rest."
95. Gen. 2:2.
96. Ex. 20:11.
97. Midrash Gen. Rabbah 10:9.
98. Ps. 23:1-2.
99. Erich Fromm, *A Forgotten Language*, p. 129.
100. Carrying from one domain to another is listed among the thirty-nine main categories of labor forbidden on the Sabbath (see above, "Thou Shalt Not!"). In order to facilitate carrying, the Rabbis introduced the concept of *Eruv*, where a "mixing" of separate domains takes place and a closeness of community is created by means of symbolic acts (see Maimonides, *Code*, Hilkhot Eruvin 1:6).
101. Ex. 20:10.
102. Samuel H. Dresner, *The Sabbath*, 1979, p. 38.
103. Ex. 31:16. *Ledorotam*, "for their generations," which is spelled in a way that could be read

ledirotam, namely "to their dwelling" or "home."
104. Deut. 11:14.
105. Thus Artur Weiser, *The Psalms, A Commentary*, Philadelphia, 1962, p. 197: "Psalm 19 consists of two independent songs, which in subject matter, mood, language and metre differ from each other so much that they cannot be composed by the same author."
106. See Scholem, *On the Kabbalah and Its Symbolism*, pp. 141-144.
107. TB Shabbat 33b; also, see Heschel, *The Sabbath*, p. 37, 109; compare P. Peli, *Shabbatot Merichot*, *Neroth Shabbat*, vol. 6, no. 128.
108. Irving Greenberg, *Guide to Shabbat*, 1981, p. 19.
109. TB Ketubot 62b.
110. TB Betza 16a.
111. Ashlag ed., Gen. p. 219.
112. Gen. 2:7.
113. This idea is expressed in the *Kiddush* liturgy. While on the festivals the concluding blessing refers to God's sanctifying Israel and the festival, which becomes sanctified through the act of Israel; on Sabbath He sanctifies the Sabbath directly and Israel is not mentioned.
114. Ex. 31:16.
115. TB Shabbat 35b.
116. Dresner, *The Sabbath*, p. 23.
117. Ex. 35:3.
118. Compare P. Peli, *On Repentance, in the Thought of Rabbi J.B. Soloveitchik*, Jerusalem, 1979, pp. 75-100.
119. *Shibolei Halaket*, 51, quoting Rashi.
120. Deut. 11:14.

121. Num. 28:9.
122. Ps. 104:15.
123. Gen. 2:3.
124. Ex. 3:2, 19:18; Jer. 23:29.
125. Lev. 6:5-6.
126. Ex. 35:3.
127. TJ Yoma 6:4.
128. Ex. 27:20-21.
129. Compare the brilliant essay on "The Aesthetic Significance of the Face," by the famous social philosopher and psychologist Georg Simmel (1858-1918, Ohio University Press, 1959): "In the features of the face the soul finds its clearest expression."
130. TB Shabbat 15a.
131. Abraham Joshua Heschel, *The Sabbath: Its Meaning for Modern Man*, New York, 1951.
132. Ex. 20:11.
133. Deut. 5:15.
134. Ex. 31:17: "It is a sign between me and the children of Israel forever."
135. Lev. 19:30: "Keep my Sabbaths and reverence My sanctuary, I am the Lord." See also Lev. 26:2 and Ezek. 22:6-8,26, 23:38 for the connection between the Sabbath-sanctuary in time and the sanctuary in space.
136. Lev. 19:3: "Ye shall fear every man his mother and his father, and ye shall keep my Sabbaths: I am the Lord your God."
137. Ex. 16:29.
138. Ex. 35:3.
139. Is. 58:13: "If thou turn away thy foot because of the Sabbath, from pursuing thy business on My holy day; and call the Sabbath a delight, and the

holy day of the Lord honorable; and shall honor it, not doing thy wonted ways, nor pursuing thy business, nor speaking thereof." For similar aspects of the Sabbath in the Prophets see also Jer. 17:19-27; Amos 8:4-7; Neh. 10:29-34, 13:16-22.

140. M. and TB, Shabbat, chap. 7.
141. TB Betza 16a.
142. TB Shabbat 119a.
143. TB Shabbat 25b; compare *Ginzei Schechter* 1, 6; Shabbat 23a; Gen. Rabbah 11; *Yalkut Shimoni*, Bahalotcha.
144. *Mekhilta*, Ki-tisa 103b; Midrash Gen. Rabbah 17,7; TB Brakhot 57b; TB Rosh Hashanah 31a. For a full development of this particular motif of the Sabbath, see Theodore Friedman, "Anticipation of Redemption," *Judaism*, vol. 16, no. 4.
145. TB Shabbat 25a, 113a; TB Ketubot 64a; Midrash Gen. Rabbah 11; TJ Peah 8,7; Midrash Deut. Rabbah, Ekev 3.
146. M. Hagigah 1:8.
147. TB Shabbat 10b; TB Betza 16a.
148. Philo, *De Opificio Mundi* 30, 43; *De Vita Mosis* 2; *De Specialibus Legibus* 2; *De Decalogo* 20; Josephus, *Against Apion* A, 122; *Antiquities*, vol. 16, 2:3.
149. Halevi, *Kuzari* 3,10; 2,50; 3,5. Maimonides, *Guide* 2,31; 3,43; 3,32.
150. Gershom G. Scholem, *On the Kabbalah and Its Symbolism*, New York, 1965, p. 139.
151. See I. Tishby, *Mishneh Hazohar* (Heb.), Jerusalem, 1961, pp. 487-90.
152. Tishby, *Mishneh Hazohar*, pp. 490-98.
153. See Gershom G. Scholem, *Major Trends in Jewish Mysticism*, New York, 1961, pp. 326 ff.

154. Mendel Bodek, *Seder Hadorot Hehadash* (Heb.), Lwow, 1865, p. 3; compare Simon Dubnow, *Toldot HeHasidut* (Heb.), Tel Aviv, 1944, p. 7.
155. See Rivkah Schatz Uffenheimer, *Hehasidut Kemystikah* (Heb.) [Quietistic elements in 18th-century Hassidic thought], Jerusalem, 1968, pp. 11-16; see also Scholem, *Major Trends.*
156. See Dubnow, *Toldot*, p. 37, where he divides early Hassidic history into three epochs: (a) origins (1740-81); (b) growth and spread (1782-1814); (c) strengthening of zaddikism and confrontation with the Enlightenment (1815-70).
157. See Dubnow, *Toldot*, p. 3.
158. For a thorough study of the impact of geography upon Hassidism, see A.Z. Escoli in *Beit Yisrael B'Polin* (Heb.), ed. Israel Heilperin, Jerusalem, 1953, vol. 2, pp. 86-141.
159. Most interesting examples of this kind are cited and documented by Raphael Mahler, *Hahasidut VehaHaskalah* (Heb.), Merkhaviah, 1961.
160. For a picture of the contemporary Jewish literary scene, see I. Zinberg, *Toldot Sifrut Yisrael* (Heb.), Tel Aviv, 1960, vols. 5-6.
161. The year of his birth was established by Rabbi Nathan Ortner in his comprehensive two-volume biography of Rabbi Zvi Elimelech, *Harebbe R' Zvi Elimelech Medinuv Zechuto Yegan Aleinu Baal Bnai Issachar, Pirkei Haiyav U'mishnato* (Heb.), Tel Aviv, 1971 (hereafter referred to as Ortner), vol. 1, p. 15.
162. See Escoli, *Beit Yisrael*, above note 158.
163. On Rabbi Elimelech and his role as founder of Hassidism in Poland and Galicia, see Dubnow, *Toldot*, pp. 178-88; also Bezalel Lando, *Harebbe R' Elimelech Melizansk* (Heb.), Jerusalem, 1963.

164. Hassidic tradition tells about many zaddikim who alluded to the time of their death by omitting to write their comments on Torah in their books on the portion of the week in which they were to die (see M. HaCohen, *Al HaTorah* (Heb.), vol. 2, Tetzaveh) or by giving other hints. They note that Rabbi Zvi Elimelech's book *Derekh Pikudekha*, which deals with the 613 commandments, stops short at the fifty-eighth mitzvah.
165. Full bibliographical listing in Ortner, vol. 2, pp. 321-84. The places in which Rabbi Zvi Elimelech's books were printed include Lwow, Munkac, Jerusalem, Safed, New York, Fernwald, Shanghai, Budapest and B'nai Brak.
166. The life and teachings of Rabbi Yaakov Yosef are the subject of *The Zaddik* by Samuel H. Dresner, New York, 1960 and of *Manhig VeEidah* by Gedaliah Nigaal, Jerusalem, 1962.
167. There are several versions of this story; see Ortner, vol. 2, pp. 359-61.
168. See note 161 above.
169. Ortner, p. 362.
170. M. Aboth 1:5.
171. Rabbi Zvi Elimelech, *Derech Mitzvoteha*, 19.
172. Quoted in many Hassidic collections, e.g. *Eser Orot* (Heb.), 23; *Ohel Naftali* (Heb.), 112; compare Ortner, vol. 2, pp. 270-71.
173. *Hosafot Meharav Zvi Elimeleh*, par. 36, quoted by Ortner, vol. 2, p. 475.
174. Various explanations are given for the choice of this rather unusual name for the book. Hassidic tradition tells that the "Seer" of Lublin "revealed" to Rabbi Zvi Elimelech that he was a descendant

of the tribe of Issachar (Ortner, vol. 2, p. 323). It seems, however, that the name is based upon the content of the book, which deals with the highlights of the Hebrew calendar. It is derived from the biblical verse: "And of the children of Issachar, men that had understanding of the times to know what Israel ought to do" (I Chron. 12:33). It alludes, of course, to the special preoccupation of the book with the subject of time. It is also interesting to note that Rabbi Zvi Elimelech's son, Rabbi Elazar, published a book named *Yodei Vinah* – continuing the verse used by his father – "men that had understanding of the times."

175. S.R. Hirsch, *Horeb*, London, 1962.
176. *The Sabbath*, p. 9; *God in Search of Man*, pp. 214-16.
177. Zohar, vol. 2, pp. 88a-b; Tishby, vol. 2, p. 5.
178. Ex. 20:8.
179. Deut. 5:12.
180. The feeling is echoed by A.J. Heschel when he writes about a people being in love with a day. In all, Heschel leans heavily, in his praise of the Sabbath, upon Hassidic sources, among which the *B'nai Issachar* occupies a central place.
181. Zohar, vol. 2 (Jethro).
182. *B'nai Issachar*, Jerusalem (offset ed.) 1968 (hereafter BIS), section on Sabbath, 1:1.
183. BIS 1:1.
184. See, e.g., *Sefer Baal Shem Tov*, Bereshith, par. 11.
185. BIS 1:1.
186. Gen. 2:23.
187. BIS 1:6.

188. M. Shabbat 2:7. English text from Danby translation (Oxford University Press), p. 102.
189. BIS 6:4.
190. Gen. 2:3.
191. Prov. 6:23.
192. BIS 20:27.
193. Zohar, quoted in BIS 3:8.
194. BIS 3:8.
195. BIS 1:12.
196. Gen. 2:3.
197. Ex. 20:8.
198. BIS 3:13.
199. Midrash Gen. Rabbah 11, 9.
200. Tishby, pp. 489-94, 501-02.
201. TB Ketubot 62b.
202. This idea stressing spiritual renewal is central to Hassidism and is elaborated on in the writings of the Great Magid of Mezrich. Compare, e.g., *Maggid Devarav LeYaakov* (Heb.), ed. Rivkah Schatz Uffenheimer, pars. 31, 73, 125.
203. BIS 7:9. The changes taking place in the Sabbath liturgy from Friday eve to Sabbath afternoon evoked many interpretations which attempt to discover the various aspects of the Sabbath; compare Tur, *Shulchan Aruch*, Orach Chayim, Hil. Shabbat 292, and Franz Rosenzweig, *Star of Redemption*, pt. 3, chap. 1 (Amir's translation, pp. 335-36).
204. *Beth Hamidrash*, vol. 1, p. 122; Zohar, vol. 2, 82b.
205. BIS 8:19.
206. Fish – Gen. 1:22; Humanity – Gen. 1:28; Sabbath – Gen. 2:3.
207. BIS 3:10.

208. TB Shabbat 118a.
209. That is, according to Rabbi Zvi Elimelech, why *ki vano vaharta* is omitted by Hassidim from the *kiddush* on Sabbath.
210. *Derech Pikudekha*, positive commandment 31.